Oh God, Where Art Thou?

Oh God, Where Art Thou?

The Great Conundrum

JAMES MCCOLLUM

RESOURCE *Publications* • Eugene, Oregon

OH GOD, WHERE ART THOU?
The Great Conundrum

Copyright © 2018 James McCollum. All rights reserved. Except for brief quotations in critical publications or reviews, no part of this book may be reproduced in any manner without prior written permission from the publisher. Write: Permissions, Wipf and Stock Publishers, 199 W. 8th Ave., Suite 3, Eugene, OR 97401.

Resource Publications
An Imprint of Wipf and Stock Publishers
199 W. 8th Ave., Suite 3
Eugene, OR 97401

www.wipfandstock.com

PAPERBACK ISBN: 978-1-5326-6491-5
HARDCOVER ISBN: 978-1-5326-6492-2
EBOOK ISBN: 978-1-5326-6493-9

Manufactured in the U.S.A.   DECEMBER 27, 2018

The *Essay on the Question of God* is philosophical opinion, and as such represent the author's personal perspectives, none of which are asserted by the author to be proven facts. The poetry and short stories are fictional. Names, characters, places and incidents are the work product of the author's imagination or are used fictitiously, and any resemblance to actual persons, living or dead, businesses, companies, events, or locations is entirely coincidental.

From Jimmy to Donna with love and gratitude:

This work would not have been possible without your support and love;

My life partner, the mother of our children, my lover, my best friend,

my inspiration and motivation to attempt to be the best person I can.

Contents

Acknowledgments | ix

Poetry | 1
    No Time for Remorse | 3
    Time Keeper | 82
    The Watchman's Gaze | 86
    Abraham's Trinity | 92
    Open Table | 97
    A Depth too Deep to See | 100
    Out of Darkness | 101
    Of Day, and Night, and God | 102
    The Wolf's Lament | 104
    Who Hears the Silence of My Sounds? | 106
    The Last Judgment | 108
    The Old Home Cemetery | 112
    Old Woman in a Chair | 115

Fiction | 119
    The Desert Beast | 121
    Dreams Beneath an Olive Tree | 135
    Sharing Tea | 147

Philosophy | 167
    An Essay on the Question of God: A Travel Journey, the Odyssey of My Mind | 169
    Prologue | 169
    Preparations | 173
    Travelogue | 174

References | 209
Resources | 211

Acknowledgments

As an initial in-depth introduction to Buddhism, I recommend readers consider investing their time in Professor Malcolm David Eckel's *Buddhism*, from The Great Courses Series. Professor Eckel's lectures helped me develop insights into the basics of Buddhism and to unravel the pronunciation of words germane to Buddhism that would otherwise have remained to me an unfathomable mystery.

As a poet, I have found John Bartlett's encyclopedic *Bartlett's Familiar Quotations*, 16th Edition, Justin Kaplan, General Editor, Little, Brown and Company, (1992), the background resource it was intended for; an invaluable tool for helping an author, or anyone for that matter, discover and trace passages, phrases, sayings and proverbs to their original sources. It provides an easy route to discover, or rediscover, the ancient texts, the Bible, the complete works of Shakespeare, and thousands of others. For a writer of fiction, a poet, a practitioner of the lost art of letter writing, this wonderous compilation of wisdom enables the researcher to subsequently go directly to the source and find the inspiration to and fuel for the imagination to refashion with new meanings and interpretations, in light of the 21st century, age old wisdom and insight into economic, social and political conditions, the psychology of the mind, the evolution of scientific discovery, and religious and spiritual insights that have fermented and given birth to heady new vintages of religious and spiritual thought, insight and criticism.

The information on our cruises, the destination ports and sites, history, and famous and often familiar locations at those ports of call, as well as information regarding the cruise ships themselves are largely derived from firsthand experiences and observations of my wife and I; our own sensory perceptions of the sights, sounds, smells, tastes and touches of our ports of call and the ships we cruised our blue earth's oceans and seas. They have also been informed by the captain's daily briefings, tour guide

Acknowledgments

expositions and stories, interaction and conversation with locals, conversations with crew members, the ship's daily itinerary sheets, internet sites such as cruise critic and YouTube, and promotional materials from the cruise lines, in particular, Royal Caribbean, with whom we have the vast majority of our approximately 240 days of cruising the earth's magnificent salt water treasures.

Poetry

NO TIME FOR REMORSE

Oh, how sweet thou art
the masters' music resurrected,
Beethoven's sonata to the moonlight
plays to comfort hearts that have bled,
while Tchaikovsky's cherubim
await the call to sing their hymn,
to soothe the senses of who; not me!
Anubis claims he has a warrant for my soul,
but the black headed jackal-man must wait.
So, too, the ferryman of the dead,
Aristophanes' spirit of the underworld, he too
will be delayed, too soon to self-congratulate
for a passage he must now retread.
And even Ra with his solar boat
sailing steadily across the daylight sky
will be held in temporary quarantine.
I have the ferry passage coins,
obols spit from copper and from bronze
that come from commerce's early dawn,
to later pay the glum old ferryman
for my soul's safe traverse to cross
the river Styx and on to Hade's gate,
where I will barter to avoid the devil's curse.
It's there I will alight to negotiate my soul's probate,
the last foreboding rail-stop along the subway line,
the check-in place for souls with burial rites complete.
But they, and Dante's fiendish hounds of hell,

and purgatory's less than pure and perfect
souls conflicted and confounded dwell,
and Paradiso's prospectus of eternal joy,
or the Buddha's freed, none-enduring self;
whatever is to be my fate, it must wait, as
my divine and tragic comedy is not complete.
They're premature, as I resist and stubbornly
defy death's dreaded, now curfewed convoy.
I hear the music, low and subtle, too soft
to startle an infant safe within its swaddled sleep.
I smell the scent of flowers; carnations, lilies
and sweet roses please my nose, as I
cast a glance to light subdued,
a tempered sky of blue, not bright,
no affront to Theia's wide shining sight.
I make no pretense, no vane self-indulged fantasy,
what awaits to be unearthed and said
will not match fabled Avon's gifted bard,
the master's magic, rhythmic, iambic verse,
much less rival his prolific, unsurpassed folios,
his craft and mastery of traits psychological,
human flaws theatrically exemplified; precursor
to Freud's insights into illusions of the mind-
subconscious, rationalized, often blind,
and yes, too, where the afflicted recognize
the tangles in their minds, and like the lady
whose hands she washes endlessly, but still
sees the blood upon her hands and to no avail
assails the damned spots that will not rub out.
Yet, still, I have words left unspoken, repressed,
languishing impatiently, anguished sentences
waiting for their moment to ascend, redressed.
And, then, I blow the ram's horn and sound
the clanging bells defiant warning;
no one come to call, not angel's yearning,
nor God's grim reaper scythe in hand,

will deny, silence or obstruct this voice of mine.
They came, the three of them unaccompanied,
all younger, a brother and two sisters,
they came, like me, from mixed stock;
Scotch and Irish sixteenth century interbred,
and later German-Swiss,
and later still from strains of Slavic blood
born in countries now vanquished from our maps.
They came from pioneer's settled land,
Connecticut's reserve in the colonial west.
They were a product of the bubbling, boiling
hot and hearty cauldron, a heady brew
the Great American experiment; toiling,
the torrid turbulent melting pot experience.
But not so great for some,
America's indigenous tribes for one,
the noble horse riders of the plains,
the plains that stretch across a continent,
east to west from sunrise to sunset,
that once was only Indian land;
and men and women with skin,
a darker shade than alabaster white,
black velvet, ebony to coffee paled with cream,
who slaved day and night for white men's dreams
of plantation crops of cotton, sugar, tobacco and rice;
and Asians with nature's most exotic eyes
creation took in envy from deep within the
peach-like fruit that almond trees produce,
who laid the rails from the Pacific West,
connecting east with west for the iron dragon
that sped across forced labor tracks;
and now, today, the Latino folk,
the ones who come from Mexico -
for work and day-long labor in fields of agriculture-
and speak the rapid Spanish tongue,
who dare deny a motley crew of narrow-minded

xenophobes their acrimonious animosities
and cross a fancied border, defying mortal danger
in silent stealth they pass the ghastly barricade,
an anti-immigration fence and gaudy wall,
a most unnatural, condescending, shameful
land-based artificial barrier reef.
Oh, how I remember vividly the flying monkeys
who served the green faced wicked witch,
now reborn in a face of orange, Oz-like,
the huckster wizard of L. Frank Baum.
He is a dangerous demagogue with an ego
that resides somewhere over the rainbow,
far out beyond reality's bounds, the space
where illusion robs reality of its grace.
He pouts and shouts it must be built,
exhibiting a condition Freud himself
would likely characterize as pathological;
psychologically unsound, unhinged, and
disconnected from reality's ordinary restraints.
He has loosed a rabid crowd, a pestilence run wild,
that with him would together build his barricade,
apparently to rival ancient China's once Great Wall,
a deep affront to our southern neighbor Mexico;
not to mention those who cannot come,
Mediterranean, the Muslim middle east, and
East Africa through the Hormuz Strait,
mothers and fathers, sisters and brothers,
children too, all because they hear and heed
the muezzin's call to pray to their God, Allah,
five times a day, they declare that God is Great.
They took the old toll road east
through the Alleghenies
my younger brother and sisters,
the road that winds and twists with lighted
burrowed holes bored out of rock and stone,
human tunnels engineered that cut through

Pennsylvania's Allegheny, Blue, Kittanning
and Tuscarora, and asks for drivers' tarot cards
that measure out a turnpike traveler's cost.
They came, these three, with
the Star Tarot card in hand,
in a quest to free themselves, to put aside
life's trivial quotidian demands, to reconnect
their souls with the rhythm of the universe,
to talk and laugh and cry in sisterhood and
brotherhood, I think, and perhaps a bit, to hear
me read and talk about my prose and poetry.
At least that is how it was, but something seems
different now, unusual I would say,
but how and why I will have to figure out.
I see my wife and children standing near,
grandchildren, brothers, sisters milling about,
soft conversations not rushed,
peppered with smiles and gentle laughs,
from ones I love and hold dear.
"Oh, they are coming now my love,"
my wife said tenderly, before she grasped
and squeezed my hand in astonishment.
Strange I think, then smile back at her,
and ask, "who is coming dear?"
I see them enter through the door,
a great Indian chief processional,
dressed in clothes adorned with artifacts
that nature in its bounty had surrendered
to the native plain riders who populate my dreams
and occupy the lines of text and noble photos
I have read and viewed with awe and reverence.
Black Elk and Crowfoot speak words without
a word about their storied chiefly roles;
headdresses adorned with eagle feathers
row after row, deer skin riding pants
and leather moccasins, shoulders strong

and bare chests, with multicolored beaded vests,
snugged across their breasts, that squaw's
deft fingers strung together during winter's long
encampment near the river's bend
below their sacred mountain's base;
the coats of arms of the noble plains-riders,
warrior class, who came with war paint on their face
to battle, what I had to ask myself.
"It's Crowfoot, son of Sitting Bull," I blurted out –
his famous father a Lakota holy man who saw a vision,
in the haze of a smoke-filled, spirit-laden dream
of a great Sioux and Cheyenne Indian alliance.
His father saw, in the tented mist, the braves astride
their appaloosa horses with bows in hand
and arrows darting through the air. He saw
his people riding to a glorious victory
that laid low General Custer
and his blue-coat, pony solider troops
down by the Little Big Horn River,
the Greasy Grass to the Lakota.
Crowfoot was first to speak with me,
first to clear the silence in the air.
"It's the flash of a firefly, my traveled friend,
this trail of life is it not," he asked, then added:
"It is the vapor of a buffalo's breath that
intrudes upon winter's cold and icy wind,
then in summer's sunset its shadow sets and
runs across the badland's grassy plains,
then fades away in the shade of approaching night
then vanishes quickly from our sight."
An eagle's feather Crowfoot offered as a gift.
I tried to grasp it in my hand
but he just placed it tight within my fingers
while I looked for my wife, and in panic said
"where is my gift for him?"
"Please, dear, I implore you, please

find my gift to him, the one I surely set aside,
the one I told you of, once, some time ago
I think, the one so vivid in my dreams,
the one residing in my mind, palpable and clear-eyed,
the one I took away with me from Lakota spirit land,
the one that duty and honor demand from me -
a fair exchange of honorable gifts
with my native American, visitor and friend.
"Another holy man," I said to my attentive wife,
"this man, too, a Lakota Sioux,
he passed this life age eighty-six.
He died at home at the Pine Ridge reservation,
an old warrior called to rest on lands ancestral,
a place ascribed by trappers, pony soldiers,
and settlers who trespassed an untamed wilderness;
the badlands are its white inspired moniker,
a vast expansive plain, home to Indian village
tee pee tents and free roaming buffalo
(in blissful spirit and in course flesh
the plains Indians natural safety net)
that move in herds of multitudes
that flow across the vast grasslands
like waves upon a rolling sea,
on sacred ground that once in time,
for centuries passing by, was treasured land
that nature had bequeathed in trust
in sacred stewardship, a lease from creation's
dawn given to the native American Indian tribes.
I recognized him, Black Elk,
second cousin to Crazy Horse,
I saw his photo in a book.
He was next, for me to greet
but how can that be, he has been gone,
dead since 1950, you see; at least that is
what a book I once read pointed out to me.
He placed a gift, a long black smoking pipe,

along my side, but once again I was foiled
and could not take it in my hands.
Bewildered, I looked toward my loving wife
and asked, "what in hell is wrong with me
that I can't reach out to receive Black Elk's pipe,
and where is my gift to exchange with him?"
She didn't seem to hear,
just gazed at me it seemed,
then she looked away toward our family.
"Despite the war paint on my face,
I come in peace my friend;
for long have you known within your soul
the peace that must come first," said Black Elk
straight out, as I assessed the man who stood
arm's length next to me with a scabbarded
hunter's knife clinging to his waist.
"Your oneness with the universe, its mysteries
and its powers, you realize, you are aware,
you have seen the vision in your dreams
like other holy men who came before.
You, too, are awake to the universal truth,
at the center dwells *Wakan-Tanka*
and the circled center is everywhere,
it dwells within each of us as we dwell
deep within the great rounded curve
of its sacred circling, mystical circumference."
"Oh, yes, I remember a discerning voice,"
I replied to my esteemed company,
"a harbinger, at the time I thought,
that once spoke these words of truth to me,
'behold this day, for it is yours to make,'
to take and shape, as an inheritor
in the face of an unsettled eternity."
"That's true, fair skinned friend,"
Black Elk replied to me, earnest and sincere,
"you have noticed truth's two faces, and what

the faces bring to you and me, and to our world;
one sad, saddled with pain and suffering,
indifferent, oblivious to our sake,
the other joyful, strong with defiant laughs,
proud mocker of the randomness of our separate fates.
But you understand, they are the same face
laughing or weeping, they are one,
they are the lighting that in contempt
illuminates a dark and stormy sky."
Basked in a sorrow he simply could not mask
Black Elk looked at me, as I nodded to his truth,
"we cry the tears of wounded souls and spirits
massacred at Wounded Knee.
A people's dream died there; it was
a beautiful dream," he said in an agonized lament.
It was a deep and unhealed wound.
It was murder, beyond doubt,
a cruel, heartless, shameful genocide
reaching back far in time, back
to a time of pristine lakes and rivers,
and clear starlit ancestral skies that compel
the gods of men to pour tears of rain
down upon the bloody hallowed ground.
"Yes, my Lakota friend," I acknowledged, and
then went on to say incredulously
"again, Black Elk, our people mourn.
The dreams of common people -
the Indian people, the Whiteman too,
and Black men and women once slaves
to white men's greed, the same pretentious ones
who stole your lands and gave the noble tribes
poisoned blankets to fight off winter's unforgiving cold;
our dreams have morphed to nightmares, our hopes
for harmony and peace again in perilous jeopardy.
You're free now, the documents and the judges
say it's so, but some within the white men's

backward tribes still deem other races a threat
and have resurrected a plague that was once,
not so long ago, in inglorious retreat, like Xerxes'
army fleeing Greece, humiliated, then beaten back
to Babylon after Salamis in consummate defeat.
Yes, today there are evil ones, cowards on the loose,
they shout and march with burning torches,
dangerous racial bigots biding purchased time,
a hazard lurking in tall weed's camouflage
waiting for the despot's scurrilous call
to rise, then wrenched from desecrated ground
the devil himself finds distasteful as burning bile
spit up from hell's raw, uncouth underbelly,
move freely like the walking dead,
to roam about, unobstructed, like vampires
unafraid of appearing in the ordinary light of day.
For a time, their sullied reputations were despised,
their bigotry and biases expertly obscured;
where once they lurked in the foggy bog
of human depravity, now they are released,
they strike with venom, a toxic hate
espousing a bigot's illusionary, poisonous ideal –
they storm and troop about our streets shockingly,
and bow in adoration to history's cunning tyrants
and the monstrous symbols they displayed,
grotesque, despotic idols marked with burning crosses
anchored to the bloodstained altar of white supremacy.
And all the while, I await, impatiently, for the devil's legions
to breach the ground and drag the hater's scorched
and ruined souls to Hade's inescapable depths,
deep within the lower reaches of descending circles
that spiral deep down in Dante's unforgiving hell.
The hope I once held for a great nation have died
again, murdered in a sordid biased hate,
spreading like the small pox that sped with lightening
speed its deadly illness through the tribes."

I shouted out, "They are condemned,"
with a running bison's thundering force,
but no one seemed to hear my angry snort.
Tears falling from his eyes, Black Elk took
a circled amulet that hung across his beaded vest,
as I just watched him place it carefully on my chest.
"You understood brother spirit," Black Elk said to me,
"you are among the common people,
you are a man who belongs as tribal kin
within the Nations, we are one, you and me."
"Many people," Black Elk said in a mournful tone,
"have forgotten their nurturing Mother Earth,
whom they now curse, and rape and rob,
and plunder savagely without care or remorse."
Crowfoot turned to Black Elk and tried to whisper
in a private conversation with his friend,
but time had dulled his hearing and he spoke
in a voice, and in his native tongue, words
that I could easily hear and surprisingly understand.
"Brother, there is a white robed man
in a land across the eastern sea; the sea
you once crossed when you were tamed and rode
a painted pony with Buffalo Bill in his wild west show.
The white-robbed one speaks with *Wakan-Tanka*,
and within a centered circle bears a wooden cross
that burns his heart for those who died so callously
in white men's acts of criminality at Wounded Knee.
I have seen this medicine man in my dreams
quite recently, he's from the spirit land,
and he has called upon the people who love
their Mother Earth, to stop the greedy and the cruel
who hoard and waste our Mother's gifts;
the soulless ones who foul the water and the air,
who steal the good earth's harvest bounty,
the hunter's meat, and leave the Nations wanting."
Black Elk turned and with Crowfoot walked away

and I looked quizzically at my wife, and said,
"I still understand, what makes him say, I understood?"
The moonlight sonata gave way to a host of cherubim
and their melodic hymn, lost on most I suspect,
who did not detect the CD's seamless switch.
Two presidents, long past and generations removed
should have startled everyone within the room,
except, no one hailed the former chiefs
or heralded in their entry with a flourish.
Mr. Jefferson and Mr. Lincoln,
came casually into the room and no one
seemed to notice or to even care.
Strange, I thought to myself, an incident so rare,
and wondered why my wife and children
did not approach or come close to me.
Surely, these great men, would draw attention;
leaders of our country, their faces so familiar,
engraved on paper currency—two and five,
and carved in mountain stone
in land that, by possession's right
and later in treaties torn to shreds,
once belonged to Crazy Horse and Sitting Bull,
and North America's continent of Indian tribes,
sovereign nations, on their own, long before
the white men came and took from them
their heritage in greed that raged inexhaustibly,
secured with money bags and bribes.
And what of Crowfoot and Black Elk,
and where are those two warriors off to now
I wondered to myself; to find a whited robbed
medicine man, or did they mean the sacred spirit
that resides within the great white buffalo?
And what twist unfurls in my dream to now
bring two men of distinguished political destiny
to travel forward to stop and talk with me?
But that is the problem isn't it;

for who can say with any certainty
the meaning that stirs within a dream?
Or, can I say in darkness interrupted, am I
a prisoner in a dream which is 'not a dream at all'?
Exhausted, giving way to emotions
I had recollected in a state of bed-ridden
tranquility, I gave up the ghost that I was wrestling
with, and acquiesced somewhat reluctantly,
accepting this is just a dream; so why not lie back,
exhale, relax, enjoy the trip, the white-robbed
medicine men dispense through a morphine drip?
"Well, truly Mister presidents, I am honored
beyond the reach of familiar words and
the meanings ordinary language can convey.
You may not know this, but I will tell you,
history's discipline pumps blood from my heart
through veins that lead into my brain,"
I said excitedly. "I have studied history
and the law, as a student and scholar,
and as practitioner of the legal trade.
I know you both through long nights,
and coffee cups, pouring over books
until my eyelids blinked and my head,
with no more room, nodded, and exhausted
gave way to sleep's narcotic relief."
"What an amazing dream, this journey
I am traveling on," I exclaimed, a child so naïve,
lost in wonderment of an impending Christmas Eve.
"This is the reason why, surely it must be,
why no one, apparently other than me,
saw the head-dressed, Lakota warrior chiefs,
and no one, despite your obvious celebrity
sees or pays either of you no mind.
Freud and Jung made much of dreams,
but I tend to be quite skeptical of those who claim
an arcane ability to find true meanings

hidden in the nuances of our esoteric dreams.
Who comes, who goes, seems to me
outside the dreamer's own control;
yet tonight you visit, and I delight
in an opportunity I sense will come but once;
that we can chat on history and philosophy
while jealous sleep is granted temporary parole,"
I said, as I let the dream unroll.
"I have questions, gentlemen, questions
that deserve answers, if ever any questions did.
I seek, I promise without resort to prosecution,
the motives in the narratives of your unfolding tales:
what thoughts perplexed your minds, what motives
pointed out your chosen paths, and served
as guides along the way, from step to last step?
What purposes, linked to righteous cause,
did you hold in firm resolve? Intuition signals me,
you each were familiar with notes from Horace' Odes;
one unafraid of frenzy from citizens who clamored
to perpetuate a wrong, and the other imperious
to the dark countenance of autocrats unchecked.
What disappointments plucked out your caring hearts,
tore at the beauty imbedded in your inward souls,
and exacted its heavy, if not grievous, deadly toll?
What where the motivations that pulsed and
pushed you down actions charged electric path,"
were just a few of the questions I asked anxiously.
"Quixotic, and quite ironic, isn't it, the two of you,"
I asked rhetorically to Misters Jefferson and Lincoln;
while both took the que and offered no response.
"One of you was educated in the classics,
a land-owning, cultured, Virginia aristocrat; and yet
you heeded Pope's refrain, kept honor in the game,
abstained from title's hereditary, and served
the public's greater good to no private end.
You were a man of privilege and of means,

all the while preferring communion with just
and righteous men, more than wealth and rich estates.
You owned slaves; humans bound in captivity,
held as private property with chattel rights attached
that lawyers with a novice skill in wills and trusts
and estates drafted legal papers to lawfully pass
your common ownership to heirs, and other nefarious
purveyors in the ghastly trafficking of human slaves."
I asked this founding father with a bit of irony:
"This is what you did, while driving revolution's course,
defending human rights and liberty, and
freedom from the evil clutch of religious tyranny,
and education for the greater public good.
Could this be the legacy of a patrician man?
A man renowned as master mason nation builder,
the wordsmith of a Bill of Grievances declaring
freedom from an English King and Parliament."
I paused then ask unsparingly, "in your knowledge
of the classics, did you never come across Josephus'
histories, and the speech he recounted of Masada
and the Jewish pledge to welcome death before slavery"?
I turned my gaze toward my other guest and said:
"Whereas you, Mr. Lincoln, were a self-educated man,
who read law books to study for the legal bar;
no mugwump you, your intellect cast
a giant shadow beyond your days in school.
Born in a humble, log cabin, an Illinois pioneer;
and if may say, a man who on sincerest principle
was among the watchful ones stubbornly opposed
from the Republics early dawn to the devil's curse
of humans held in chains with lives bound round slavery.
I can only speculate as there is no record
I can footnote or find a resource to, but you
must have drawn solace in one stanza gleaned
from James Russell Lowell, for you, yourself,
were not enslaved, silenced, nor afraid to speak.

You placed your highest duty to save a nation
from dissolution, to lead an adolescent union
through its time of gravest travail, fighting off
an armed revolution where brother's blood
flowed like rivers over battlefields won and lost,
in a most uncivil murderous mutiny.
You were its reluctant savior who grasped
in his strong hands and stopped the miscreants'
raised meat clever from cutting clean in half
our country on bloody insurrection's butcher's block."
"It's true," I continued, "the divisions have been slow
to mend, and bitterness lingers still, like spoiled meat,
sixteen decades since, while an army of once dead
bodies, a putrid pestilence not fully decomposed,
rises from the bloody ground and chants ugly,
loathsome slogans that fiends and human monsters
crafted long after you, like Caesar, fell, and treason's
bloody tracks besieged our country's soul."
"Oh," I said, to ease the moment of intensity,
as if it weren't a matter of common knowledge,
as a casual farmer might say 'that's good'
when a cow gives birth to a healthy calf,
"you were also U. S. presidents,
who in the White House proudly stood."
"Now, please tell me Mr. Jefferson,
I beg your indulgence sir, I ask
what were the hallowed causes trapped
within your complicated state of mind,
a mind of calculation, calm and imperturbable?
What passion of necessity gave signal to some
distant voice that stirred your soul and sparked
a vocation dedicated to the greater public good?"
"It's true, I know," I said quickly
before President Jefferson could demure.
"Much has been written about you,
which I'm sure you are well aware.

You, yourself, were quite prolific
and wrote extensively. No disrespect intended sir,
the quality I seek to ascribe was as a writer,
given to what Faulkner may have said it best -
to be graced with the purpose and the privilege
of helping man and our endangered species endure
that other generations might have life to live and love.
You were so unlike Mr. Lincoln, in one regard for sure;
though no less wise and admired, he tended
to be stingy with the words that formed the lines
and defined his speeches and his written papers.
He often parceled them in small tight bundles,
literary treasures his speeches and his letters,
pure genius at work in eloquent brevity."
"You are correct, I admit," replied Mr. Jefferson,
"I have written quite extensively throughout my life.
Let me think a moment, so I can be concise.
I want to give Mr. Lincoln time to state his case
and stay within the limits of your wandering dream,
and give to others their time, too, that they might
step inside the intimacy of your unsettled sleep
before reality intrudes to awaken you."
Jefferson, no friend of the priestly class,
looked dubiously at the circled amulet,
Black Elk, before departing, had placed
upon my chest. "Your *spirit journey*," he said,
"I believe is what I overheard the Indian chief
say to you just before he took his leave."
"Now, it's well known I wrote my own epithet.
My headstone speaks for me and tells visitors
what was primal to my soul and most important
in my life; what pushed my mind and inspired,
if that's the word, my soul's driving quest
to leave this earth a better place that men
might be free in their pursuit of happiness."
The white-haired Virginian was a congenial

cultured man, well dressed and manicured.
He was a master of the written word
but less so, it was said, in public speech;
although I must say I was not surprised
with the ease he displayed in civil discourse.
There was no rancor in his voice when we engaged
in partisan debate, and I applauded his belief
that progress does not happen in politics or life
within its most meaningful moments without
pragmatic compromise—a fact, a practiced art,
that recently has lapsed, now consigned
to hard, unyielding, fallow ground,
seemingly impossible to resurrect.
I wondered again to myself, and looked
toward my wife. I quizzed her, asking why
everyone was standing, appearing to be casting
downward glances, while meanwhile, I confess,
I was delighted with the cast of unexpected visitors.
Oh, well, I thought to myself, what can you
or anyone expect from a sleeping man's dream?
"You are a complicated man, Mr. Jefferson."
"You can forgo the formality, just call me by my name;
Thomas, as it was given, is fine enough by me,"
said the country's third president lightheartedly.
"Most who view the declaration that you drafted
for the Continental Congress as a masterpiece
of prose, but I have read and reread the initial draft
which to me reads more poetically, pure and powerful,
original in its craft, like genius strokes of paint
from the brush of master Michelangelo.
So here is a question for you, sir, did you write
your draft in prose or was it poetry? "Well, yes,
I guess it might have been the case
that I had the meter of poetry in mind,"
said an originalist, the storied lead author
of our country's seminal, sacred text.

"I wanted the King of England, to read the words
as if they were drawn from a rhythmic sonnet
penned by England's fabled favorite son,
William Shakespeare come alive in mimicked words
and actor's speech that cause the king to flinch.
That's bitter irony, I thought, adding rightful insult
on to injury to the English king. But traditionalists
within the gathered representatives held sway;
more conservative in style, in this political foray,
they insisted that the document reflect
a more familiar, tightly crafted prose.
The declaring document, they pressed,
must be truer in style to the English Magna Carta –
it must paint a picture of a regal rose,
a crimson flower, a beauty that will not die.
For this, they in earnest said, would declare
in statutory words a new American covenant,
a binding contract with mutual rights and obligations
clearly stated and carefully shared between
and among the people and its new government.
They prevailed on that account, but I held out
insisting stubbornly to include within the grasp
of democracy' holy writ a novel concept
in that evolutionary epoch in time's long march;
a fundamental tenant, one essential reason
for a government to exist—that men might pursue,
without a government's overreach, their own
unencumbered path to peace and happiness.
I also lost an author's constant give and take,
the literary battlefield with his editors who always have
the final word regarding lines that die along the way,
and I was forced to acquiesce, as colleagues
less radical than me replaced the stronger
more encompassing 'inherent' with 'certain'
in the recognition of rights held unalienable.
It was, I admit rather shamefully, another battle

fought and lost to the Gordian Knot of slavery;
for the word *inherent* would have captured slaves
within its fundamental all-encompassing set, a price
many among the congress feared and dread."
"I have to ask you sir, you authored words that
stirred men's souls, declaring that all men
are created equal, and yet to my bewilderment,
you incongruously denied so-called environmentalists
who claimed that climate and place determined
why northern European white was the superior race.
You said that native Indians were equal in intellect,
but called for them to be removed from tribal lands
to places where they could be taught white men's ways,
stripped of their ancestral habitat they would assimilate
and join the white man's tribes of the highly civilized.
And equally, outrageously, you were a trafficker
of black Africans, yourself an owner
of men and women slaves; captured human beings
who labored for your gain, involuntarily,
bound in servitude to work out their precious lives
in your household or in fields upon your estates.
You were a good and well-intentioned man,
but how can you explain that I might understand
this fundamental, disarming, disconnect?"
"It's fair to call me out, and yes, to justly criticize;
but do try to place me properly within the epoch
of my time. I seek no pardon for my transgression
against humanity. I ask only for mitigation
and forgiveness, for early on I did not look
hard enough to embrace the obvious proofs
that nature had given to our Black and Indian
brethren, talents equal to those of Whites."
Mr. Jefferson paused for a moment; then relief
followed quickly after, as he emancipated
his troubled soul, a stilled and quiet conscience
no more, unburdened in an unmasked act

of sincere regret, a true confession,
borne out in words of deep contrition;
"no person living wished more genuinely than I,
to eradicate the doubts, I once entertained
and expressed regarding the natural intellect
allotted to blacks by creation, only later, in shame,
to acknowledge in all respects in the mystery
of creation blacks are no different from ourselves."
"And what of the native American Indian tribes,"
I pushed back forcefully, "did you not once
state their alleged ferocious barbarities
might justify extermination of a race?
Do you not know the history of genocide
that ultimately ensued and burned a scarlet letter
of disgrace upon our country's soul? For genocide took
our nation's native Indians down from five million strong
to a few hundred thousand as the Nineteenth Century
rushed away through time's relentless revolving door."
It was clear to me that I had wounded Mr. Jefferson.
I put an arrow straight within his troubled heart,
and fearing that my guest would leave I took mercy
on my visitor and said, "do not be too harsh
or quick to self-abuse for we come
to this life reluctantly, with no guarantees
to draw a single breath at the birthing moment
and no assurances another breath will follow;
fragility is our common carrier, or constant companion,
and only the greatest of souls, fanatical in purpose,
transcend the conventions of the time
and place into which they are born."
History's judges have been generous to you.
Mr. Jefferson, historians hold you in high esteem,
they applaud your role as a crowning intellect among
the founding fathers of our nation's great experiment.
This is history's en banc judgment, made without
glossing over the undisputed fact that you had slaves,

and more recently the science of DNA evidence
that you sired children with a slave. So, I ask you sir,
I'll take you at your word. Do you deny the evidence
that supports the charge you failed your debt
to marriage owed to an underage slave girl?"
I renewed the prosecutor's role and asked:
"was she not the Heming's girl, a slave
who traveled on your European diplomatic trips,
and who was a slave owned by and whom
in time you inherited from your wife; a child
grown to womanhood, whom records show
you owned until your death? Now, how
in good conscience did you not free,
not emancipate this servant intimate to you?"
"In my defense," Thomas Jefferson protested,
"I was truly fond of her, and never again married
after my one and only dear wife's now forgotten death."
Then with a skilled politician's art of a boxer's
bob and weave, Thomas Jefferson danced away
strategically from the topic of my probing inquiry.
"The law, as you well know, is often inconclusive,
only in the most egregious cases unshakable,
clearly black or white; more often guilt
or innocence plays out in jurors' minds
tangled up in greyer shades of nuanced greys.
That's why I placed such faith in a jury of citizens.
I believed it better for a panel to deliberate
liability, culpability, innocence or guilt.
This approach was superior, in my suspicious mind,
to the prospect of a single judge, one person
too easily compromised, individually suspect,
susceptible and corruptible to the intoxicating
allure of unrestrained judicial might,
denying to the accused the voices
that natural right has vested in his peers."
"I admit my failing," lamented Mr. Jefferson,

"I should have done more. I should have freed
all the slaves I owned. I admit, none more deserved
her shackles broken off than sweet Sally, my love.
I should publicly have condemned this grievous trespass,
that men and women, and children, too,
were given over, chained to slavery foul and cruel.
This moral failure to condemn is the ghastly price
that accrues with compound interest for those
who stood in silence while generations
of innocents bore the scars of slavery.
I should have loosened the grip I held so tight,
to narrow the publication of my *Notes on Virginia*.
I should not have tried to hide my thoughts,
obscure my beliefs so extensively
from the reading publics' close review.
That was an overreach I truly do regret.
My writings, I acknowledge apologetically, might
have inspired others with more strength of character
than me, to put conviction into practice, but shamefully
I asked the *Notes* to be closely held, not shared,
for I felt trapped, ensnared in a coward's
loathsome net of self-imposed confining fear.
I was, in retrospect, afflicted with a faint-hearted
dread of suicidal martyrdom, a holy cross
I could not mount. I had not, I admit, Hamlet's claim
that conscience made a coward out of me,
and for this grievous trespass alone,
I have died a thousand crucifying deaths.
I did call it out in writing, that statemen who permit
half its citizens to trample on the rights of the other,
transform the exploiters into demons and despots,
and the exploited into righteous enemies,
who are then confined to hell where all are punished
unforgivingly to wage barbaric wars eternally.
I understood, but failed my moral obligation
to God, to country, and to human kind.

I called it unsavory, but failed to act upon conviction,
as if villains came to be, out ruinous necessity.
I should have spoken out in open public discourse
that no person would choose a country in this world,
our new nation included, over a place where unshackled
they would be born free to live and labor for themselves."
"Alright, Mr. Jefferson," I acquiesced,
"let's leave the topic of slavery
for Mr. Lincoln to more fully address."
"You lived in perilous times, Thomas Jefferson,
and the challenges that plagued your time
have come full circle to haunt this country's soul.
Immigration, religion and the scare of dictatorship
now perplex and test the mettle and resolve
of our grand experiment of democracy in the raw."
"I know what you speak off," Mr. Jefferson replied.
"I wrote in private letters to Richard Henry Lee in 1778
that emigrants from the Mediterranean, with their skills
in agriculture and other arts would be of greater value
to nation building then more of Northern European
whites who had settled here in large numbers,
overwhelming race, and culture, and traditions;
an obstacle to the opportunity for diversity to expand,
and to enrich posterity's human pool of genes.
I said in my letters to Mr. Lee that with this mix
of Mediterranean stock our country would be better off,
much more advanced in our production of silk and oil
and wines, especially wine. For other than abstinence,
I do believe, only wine can tame hard liquor's
injurious effects on rough cut common folk.
For I do believe that the working labor class
are too easily encumbered and impaired
under the scurrilous influence of whiskey's spell.
I am convinced that grapes harvested from the vine
are close to divine and far less prone to dull
and addle, and less deleterious to addicted minds.

It should be true, despite a lack of direct evidence,
that God himself implored to us that we
should bring to him a beaker of wine, fresh
from the presses of grapes crushed by the feet
of servant's faithful to their master's call."
Then old Tom Jefferson, with a gentle rise
of his eyes remarked: "all my affairs were settled
for that approaching time, but I did have one
unfilled death-bed request, that near my departing
leave, providence grant to me just one more sip
of divine, delicate, and satisfying dry red wine."
"You did mention," asked Mr. Jefferson
"religion now perplexes the country's soul?"
"Yes, there are evangelicals, Christians,
fundamentalists insisting, we were created
as a Christian nation, first and fundamentally,
and that consequently, Christianity is the basis,
the linchpin of all our laws and government policies,
and other faiths by implication, are secondary
and lack the legal standing to guarantee protections,
equal within the clear and present language
of the Constitution's commonly constructed
original intent, and secured in subsequent
judicial interpretations of its reach and limitations.
It is a perilous tack that today judges must
map out contours of the intent of originators
centuries removed from the insights drawn
within the minds of men, who with all due
and appropriate respect, would be deemed mad
if, at that original time, professed belief that one-day
man might fly and soar above the clouds, or walk
upon the moon, or deploy malignant weapons
born beneath the ground, that when unleashed
from secret holes of hell and in a second's flash,
enables one grim reaper, a lesser being
than a fallen angel cast into hell, to push

a trigger button and usher in the end of man.
This great conflagration comes in a rush,
and in preemption terminates lonely man's
lease of space on planet earth."
"Well," said Thomas Jefferson quite miffed,
"I presume you are aware that I also drafted
a Bill for Establishing Religious Freedom,
presented to my Virginia House of Delegates,
that this progressive state with liberty
on its mind eventually passed into law."
I nodded in acknowledgement, "you cared greatly
on this matter; it's hard to miss, it's engraved
on your headstone, Mr. Jefferson, isn't it?"
"It's an impious presumption of the ruling class,
civil and religious, who attempt to dominate
the exercise of faith. It is tyranny unchecked;
our civil rights have no dependence on beliefs,
be they on religion, science or the arts,"
was his impassioned, adamant response.
"On this fundamental issue," said Jefferson
with conviction and with force, "I'm proud
of my actions. I did not stand by in the shadow
of the gnarly trunk of a giant, ancient oak tree,
or seek cover beneath the shade cast by limbs
as thick and colossal as brontosaurus legs.
I waged a public fight, with crucial help
from Madison and others, and as brothers
bound by sweat and blood to a patriotic cause,
my beloved Virginia rendered unto man and God
forbearance of the will and freedom from coercion,
proclaiming from thence on into perpetuity
that no man should be compelled to frequent
or imbibe a religious worship, or of place
or ministry whatsoever, nor shall be enforced,
restrained, cajoled, molested, or burdened
in his person or his property, or suffer other

consequences upon his religious opinions
or beliefs; and all men shall be free to profess,
and by argument maintain, their opinions
and beliefs, including those who cast doubt
on religion's tantalizing fundamental efficacy,
and in doing so, in no way shall affect,
jeopardize or enhance their fundamental rights,
civil or religious all the same, guaranteed
within freedom's innate and elemental capacities."
Mr. Jefferson punctuated his sympathies
on religion and the state with a boldface
exclamation point, "the separation of religion
from the state must be absolute, inviolable,
like the shepherd herder who works hard
to keep separate his goats and sheep,
on this to death there can be no compromise!"
"My time has run over, as the time keeper
prepares to ring the bell to end the final round
of this intriguing bout, and give to Mr. Lincoln,
who has listened patiently, his rounds to spar
with you before the referee counts out to ten.
But first, I have a warning I must register;
it's a caution from the scars of others
who have learned, and we should heed.
I heard you raise a frightening specter,
the crowning bane of a true democracy,
the tyranny of a dictator's dark agenda,
for once on board a hungry tiger the devil
despot cannot but to death dismount.
Of all the wild beasts loosed from hell,
Ben Johnson pled, preserve us from a tyrant
with all the dark archangel's attendant deviancies.
Oh, we must stop him in his cleft hooved path
before in infamy he has the final loathsome say
that undermines faithful citizens' rights and liberties,
destroys the common good, and covers natural law

in a deathly shroud; freedom's mortal enemy,
as the dark prince pursues absolute political command
in the devil's dirty hand of corruption and control.
"That's correct, Mr. Jefferson," I said earnestly.
"That is a concern, more accurately a threat;
some of us have the opinion that our democracy
is in danger, imperiled by a leader who speaks
and acts as if he were a king, seated on a throne,
standing above and beyond the ordinary reach
of the rule of law that naturally applies to all."
Mr. Jefferson turned and stared, his eyes
in undivided attention riveted on me.
"The gravest dangers to our liberty lurk within
the tumult of the tyrant's claim of necessity.
Are you familiar with many scripture passages?"
he asked not waiting for an answer.
"There is a passage, I seem vaguely to recall,
that we can resurrect and modernized restate.
So, let me try my best: let the ram's horn sound
a high alert, its baleful sound a warning
to unsuspecting citizens of an imminent attack,
a Defcon 1, in modern parlance, I believe,
for this day's nuclear missile dogs of war."
I answered rather sheepishly, "yes, I think so,"
knowing, unlike Holmes and Pierrot,
I truly hadn't the vaguest inkling of a clue.
"Then blow that damned horn, sound the alarm.
Do not allow a self-absorbed, self-righteous,
drunk on power, greedy despot, the space he needs
to pierce the beating heart of our democracy.
Heed Locke's admonishment, that tyranny's rise
signals clear the laws precipitous demise.
Do not cede your liberty to such greedy fiends,
hold fast the door or before the dawn
of some early day, the blood suckers will,
with a surgeon's skill, slice and sever

precious arteries, and the blood of kinsmen
and of patriots will spurt in a fatal gush
of holy sacrificial blood, while their rupture
will be tolled with woeful bells of doom.
And generation following generation,
filled with the ranks of noble sacrifices,
even unto death - patriotism's most irrefutable self -
will shout out their infamous betrayal:
'We stood against the gathering storms,
our blood was spilled, in savagery;
our souls were darkened; our minds
forever damaged, that rights and liberties
would not be lost to powers perverse,
thunderbolts wielded by tyrants and despots,
and dictators with claims of crisis—a deadly bacterium
concocted in a secret laboratory petri dish,
or genuine, the difference does not matter
when lies are spawned, and fake news spins
the despot's propaganda tune, and false words
infect minds in flight from reason, fleeing in full retreat.
It's a poison deadlier 'than a mad dog's tooth',
said the Abbess, in what to me seems not a comedy
of errors, but a most unfortunate tragedy."
"Oh, it's perilously true," asserted Mr. Jefferson;
"as a wolf howls in broad daylight, obscured
in sheep's clothing, the hidden beast inside
trumpets false assertions of necessity,
while treachery and treason await,
a sure and certain path to tyranny."
Finally, Mr. Lincoln had his opportunity;
he seized his tardy opening, like a general
acting on the turning fortunes of a battle,
who overcomes a long-delayed opportunity
for some sign to gain strategic advantage
from the miscalculations and misfortunes of war.
"Mr. Jefferson is right, I this know personally.

Amid our nation's greatest crisis,
I had my rendezvous with destiny.
A solemn task and grave responsibility
fell to me, a humble servant from the plains.
Responding like a doting parent to an infant country's
fearful cry, I bore the trust to lead our nation,
to fight off treason's spawn, to save, if providence
was real, our adolescent democracy, to protect
and to ensure the very survival of a system
of self-governance, a trinity of co-equal powers,
where judges and legislators stand in equilibrium
with presidents elected, by citizens who patriotically
cast election ballots, and from a slate of candidates
give voice to the people's choice for whom
shall be elected the country's chief executive.
As the country's president, my duty was unalterably
to work within the boundaries of our sacred text -
a document proscribing individual rights
and liberties, with limitations placed upon
an errant government's zealous overreach.
I called on God's mercy to stop a cancer
spreading quick, set with sharpened teeth
to eat its own children if it must. Oh, God,
the merciful I cried out, no badge of courage
in the face of war; protect us from another
fallen angels' insurrection, this one hatched
among the Union's southern slavery-loving states.
I knew that blood must flow to stave off nature's
condemnation, to further reason's growing call
that all, means all, when we do solemnly declare
that all men, nature's rainbow of humanity,
are created equal, in fact, and before the law."
I said, "that is the essence of the foreboding message
you delivered to Congress, that fourth of July 1861."
Secession was a threat to the fate of more
than us. The whole family of man, you plunged ahead,

is presented with this quintessential question:
'whether a constitutional republic, or a democracy –
a government of the people, by the same people –
can, or cannot, maintain its territorial integrity,
against its own domestic foes.'"
"And now," with anger rising in my voice,
I said, "our beloved country is threatened, crazed
advocates of arms walk about with hand guns
holstered on their hips, and military rifles
that shoot out bullets fifty rounds a minute
are slung over the shoulders of shouting men
and women, confirming that hell has loosed
its assembled parasites and that Paradise is lost.
These homicidal zealots carry assault weapons
made for the dung of war, designed for soldiers'
use to kill in horrifying gore; witness to a regiment
of foes laid down in quick time march to fall
and die on blood-soaked battle grounds.
These para-military thugs spew hatred
and open bigotry, and walk about in day's
unobstructed light. Emboldened and enflamed
by leadership defamed, these malcontents
proudly display two symbolically repulsive flags:
one commemorates the south's rebellious,
futile, dying last gasp to save a slavery system
it would not in peace put aside, while the other
symbolized a monstrous genocidal Nazi plague.
There are miscreants marching in our streets,
parading defiantly on our public squares,
while ministers of God, afflicted with a flawed
but all too common moral lapse, fuel
a mob insanity, blaming others aligned
outside their crazed cults of worshipers
for every tragedy and natural calamity.
They incite their followers to tread in anger,
and in fury, uncontained, trample imagined enemies,

and then these malcontented ministers of hate
absolve the guilt of those whose clothes
are sprinkled with the blood of innocents.
Despicable and deplorable, these purveyors
of religious bigotry claim that a good, just, loving
and compassionate God is offended grievously
by the dazzling rainbow palette of human diversity.
And, that in just consequence, God himself
in revenge and retribution has directed nature's
recurring, capricious natural calamities, upon a sinful,
depraved, cursed humanity; the same humanity
he created with his hands, in likeness to himself,
so, say, in sermons unhinged, his narrow minded,
science-denying, bigoted, ministers of hate."
Mr. Lincoln shuttered in disgust, while Mr. Jefferson
just shook his head back and forth repeatedly,
in silent misery deploring religion's dark hiding place.
"I have to ask you sir, as I did with Mr. Jefferson,"
I said to Mr. Lincoln, "although personally
opposed to human slavery, you too,
are not free of history's careful scrutiny."
"I suspect," replied the 16th president defensively,
"you refer to what I said of slavery and how
I balanced that injustice against the imminent
prospect of the Union's disembodiment and death?"
"Yes sir, that's one of two," I replied.
"Well," tall, gangly and looking weary still,
Mr. Lincoln said without further hesitation,
"I said that nothing was more important to me
than to save the Union and to uphold
our constitution, the sentential that stands
in defense of our experiment with democracy.
I said, and I meant it earnestly, if I could
abolish slavery everywhere within our country,
and if that would save the imperiled Union,
then duty demands that is what I must do.

I also said, that if I could abolish slavery only
among the rebellious states, and if that would
save the Union, then that is the action
that duty mandates I must undertake.
And if I, in troubled conscience, determined
I could save the Union only by leaving
slavery intact; then as president, I reluctantly
admit that is what duty compels me to do.
For in the end, I truly did believe that human
progress, like the railroads coming change
to commerce, would soon render human slavery
obsolete, but only if our Union first survived;
and that was an inconvenient truth, the agonizing
tortured middle path from which emerged
my presidential proclamation emancipating
some, but not all of America's slaves."
"I have another question, sir, one that troubles me,
one that Mr. Frederick Douglass, late your friend,
pointed out to you. He roundly criticized you,
that you could somehow think the nation's
four-million slaves might be freed only to be
exiled and colonized somewhere off our soil,
somewhere outside, beyond the land
they were chattels to, indentured, their toils
enduring until their last labored breath."
"Mr. Douglass' voice inspired others to speak out
in clear contempt of that specious thought."
I did not relent and pressed on, "the *Liberator*
castigated you for the mere suggestion of colonization,
pointing out that the slaves 'are as much as natives
of the country as any of their oppressors,'
calling your attention to the unassailable fact
that it was here, not distant lands far offshore,
where most slaves were born, all be in captivity."
Mr. Lincoln nodded in sad acknowledgement,
"I bear the *Liberator's* harshest criticism, a truth

that lanced my heart, as I too lately came to realize
how unconnected I was to black men, free and slave
and their attachment to this country, and their horror
and revulsion that this nation, claiming refuge and relief
to the world's oppressed, would ever consider removing
the entire population of blacks to a distant shore,
be it Central America or colonial Africa.
Oh, the songs of slaves still hurt my ears
and haunt my mind; their prayerful testament
to Almighty God for their deliverance
from the chains of involuntary servitude
are a yoke that I must carry everywhere.
Not my finest day, a painful and shameful
groan I share with Mr. Jefferson, doubting
that blacks had the capacity, held back
in slavery's taint of opportunities repressed,
to integrate, assimilate into our country's quilt.
And I, like him before, deeply do regret
this shortsighted, biased disregard."
"Mr. Lincoln, please do not mistake the questions
for a corner's inquiry, as they are no more
than a quest of mine, consumed like Howard Carter's
stubborn search for Tutankhamen's lost tomb
that ultimately was discovered accidently
buried under rubble in the Valley of the Kings.
There is blame enough for all of us to share
and still much prejudice and bigotry to overcome.
You, like Mr. Jefferson, are admired and revered,
to many you are our country's finest president; so,
as I said to Mr. Jefferson, don't be unduly harsh
and unforgiving of yourself, for nothing my friend,
if I might call you so, beyond the air we breathe
is given to any of us, and history cannot fairly extract
you entirely from the machinations and imperfections
of your chance encounter of place and time.
Human bondage is a pestilence, an abomination,

its dark shadow eclipsing God and nature;
and still I'm distraught to say, its cold wind burns
the exposed skin of mankind's composite soul.
Today, man still fails, bequeathed as fallen angels
forever condemned to groan and moan in pain,
banished to hell for mutiny against authority.
Slavery might have morphed to altered forms,
but its ugliness takes on new embodiments
as human trafficking ensnares young girls
and boys, trapped, prisoners in cramped,
dangerous, foul air, unsanitary, sweat shops,
and, worse yet, in abhorrent sexual servitude."
I paused to let the news take its full effect, then said:
"I know that time tugs earnestly on your long coat tails,
but I beg you for one more insight, an artifact
from history resurrected for instruction,
if not too late, today: a leadership trait
and strategy that you deftly employed,
that just might help our imperiled country
rediscover fundamental purposes it has lost,
before its current leaders take us spiraling down
Mr. Lewis Carroll's rabbit hole, to a madness
and insanity, it will not, before collapse, escape."
"Ask, I'll do my best," responded Mr. Lincoln.
"We have a president surrounded by a cabinet
of men and women, many ill-equipped if not unfit
(as has been said for the head of state as well)
to lead the government's departments—the organs
of the body politic that guide essential services
and provide protections, foreign and domestic.
Each fawning cabinet minister is called upon to read
from briefing books prepared specifically, to praise
this fragile man for doing things that he invents
as accomplishments, and later at rally's and events,
reminiscent of those dangerous times of a rising tide of
of insidious Hitlerian fascist minds, incites his followers

with choleric propaganda, poison filled with willful
bogus claims, fact-less fabricated crafty lies."
Mr. Lincoln looked at me and said, "how can I help?"
"Well, a book has been written, by a respected historian,
a woman of percipient insight, a Pulitzer Prize master
of the written word. She credits you for a genius
architectural design, no imitation for inspiration,
no precedent for your cabinet enterprise
built of strong, outspoken talents; a 'team of rivals'
was the project label she heaped praised upon."
"Yes," replied Mr. Lincoln, "there were many skeptics
expressing serious doubts regarding my approach.
Many thought my cabinet would be an incongruent,
unmitigated mess. There are dangers in such discord,
they warned. So many were incredulous, sure
the plan was born to fail leadership's demanding test,
and in short term fall and miss the mark
of effective executive command. But I knew
instinctively, I did not need men who saw
the painted strokes of master's paintings
exactly through my eyes, or read and interpreted
as I, the psychological compulsions of characters,
the poetic ebb and flow, the often-tragic turns
of Shakespeare's plays detailing human tragedies.
Nor did I need men who looked cowardly toward
a weather vane - as if it were a divining tool,
a modern Theban oracle - before they rendered
unto me and to our country, their unencumbered,
unrestrained best counsel and advice."
"I did not seek consent from men confined
to a common theme. I chose the strongest men,"
said Mr. Lincoln, "because I had no other right and duty.
It would have been the folly of a small-minded man
to deprive the country desperate in its need
of the services of men as smart or better
yet much smarter and experienced than I.

That is what the country needed most,
and notably should expect, no less,
from its president; that the American President,
must embrace their moral power to cancel
vanity's captivity of self-indulgence, and avoid
the trap that greed lays out for interests
that are personal and stand as obstacles
to their duties to the public's greater good.
Think, they must unfailingly, only of the country's
most imminent needs, and what benefits can
the government best provides to its citizens
even if it leads to personal loss, a majority's
rejection of their policies and ultimately
to their political demise, for the same fair
and honest duty any subject owes its country,
belongs no less to its elected president.
Is that not what we ask, even so much more,
from our soldiers whom we call upon to die,
to make the ultimate sacrifice, in selfless service
to preserve the country from the wild beast
of tyranny, and uphold its cherished belief
in a fundamental set of constitutional promises,
a sacred covenant defined by declarations of equality;
God's sanctified enduring quest for freedom's holy grail.
This is clearly and convincingly, unequivocally,
beyond any reasonable doubt a doubting Thomas
could construct, democracy's fundamental
promissory note: to protect an individual's freedom
to pursue in their own unalienable way, to navigate
and discover their individual path to happiness,
a right creation in liberal generosity accords
to sensate beings, a path that must be free
from government overreach—the always present
threat of dangerous tentacles regimes deploys
to rein in those who venture out to freedom's edge,
and a path the law must guard and protect,

that no majority in power misuse advantages
they accrued and never place at risk,
unlike the noble savior strung up, spread out
upon a wooden cross by authorities and the rich
who each and every day would, if they could,
trample under foot our sacred rights, obstruct
the freedoms we acclaim, and suppress and
shutter the aspirations of vulnerable minorities."
All eyes turned toward two men just arrived,
one bound to a small, plain, horseless, metal chariot,
the other propelling the sturdy carriage forcefully
from behind, like a magic carpet flying through the air.
And all the while, no one seemed to notice much
less care that Jefferson and Lincoln were gone,
replaced by two Roosevelts: one from Sagamore Hill,
the other from Hyde Park, family owned patrician homes;
one at Oyster Bay near Long Island Sound,
the other near Poughkeepsie, a country refuge north
of metropolitan New York City - the grand estates
of Theodore and Franklin Delano, respectively.
One follows another, president after president,
like elephants in cars that ride the iron rails
and later parade in circus tents pitched in towns
along the railroad's path, while hawkers line
the midway spouting promises of medicinal
cures for all that ails and troubles human kind.
They come and go, intruders in my dream,
these temporary inhabitants of a great white house
on Pennsylvania Avenue, our D.C. Capital,
not far from marble memorials that honor
Presidents Jefferson and Lincoln, recently departed,
now presidents-in-exile from my relentless dream.
'Hell', I said randomly to no one in particular,
"if they could hear, I'd shout, I'd scream,
but it's my dream not theirs, and my wife and family
just stand and talk, and hug each other lovingly

while I have presidents who come and stay,
and then quickly pass unnoticed from the scene,
like the formerly invisible Indian chiefs."
Presidents Roosevelt, ponder this aspect,
distant cousins, fifth degree, while Eleanor,
Franklin's wife was Theodore's little niece.
Theodore was the stocky one with barrel chest
and full mustache, pushing Franklin like Pharaoh
warrior kings riding to battle on a chariot.
Both wore wire rim spectacles that Franklin's
portraits sometimes showed, unlike the braces
on his legs that he and a deferential press
tacitly agreed they'd never unnecessarily print
a comment on or purposefully portray in a photograph.
"I know our time is limited," said I mercurially.
"Dreams are fragile interludes that fade
without consent, and leave us wanting,
unfulfilled and frustrated with the fact
their time is just too damned short
to sort things out and maybe get it right."
"I know you both; well, yes, I admit
that's from books I have read zealously,
not from interaction, not a bona fide experience.
But worker's rights, and a safety net for struggling
folk tangled in the deadly widow's spider's web
that lays in wait at the fragile edges of life's
sustaining atmosphere, and your calls for freedom
from monopoly and the greed of corporate personhood,
were values that you shared and championed politically.
Theodore, you created a national conservatory,
a jewel box with natural wonders locked inside
and gave the public in the large the precious keys
to unlock posterity's access to the golden box,
America's own Ark of the Covenant.
You were a true protector from the onslaught
of the unrelenting tyranny of greed, assuring

natures gift to all—plants and animals,
mountains, plains, lakes and rivers, too,
were locked away secure from plunderers
whose avarice had no restraint, no patriotic
bounds, and signed into law a congressional lease
of power to the president to preserve, as conservator
of our heritage, our ancient aboriginal reserves –
America's natural treasury of ancestral antiquities.
When angels failed to keep safe the sacred sites,
you secured the lawful granted authority to proclaim,
without congressional approval on federal ground
national monuments and historic sites, and saved
for posterity two hundred thirty million acres
in a national trust appended to the public's land.
You expanded California's Yosemite—its giant sequoia
rising to up heaven's door, and the great cascading
falls that poured down from melting winter snow.
You collared Oregon's collapsed volcano's Crater Lake,
and Colorado's Mesa Verde where within Cliff Palace
dwelled the ancient tribal people we know as Pueblo.
You protected the river Platt, Antelope Springs
and the Little Niagara, where the Choctaw
and the Chickasaw gave to our nation six hundred
acres of Platt Indian reservation land to preserve
the health of nature's fresh, restoring mineral springs.
You designated what was once Lakota land
in the Dakotas, North and South—Wind Cave
and Sullys Hill national parks, with calcite honeycomb
caverns underground, and Spirit Lake Reservation's
wildlife game preserve. You earmarked eighteen
national monuments we now cherish: including
Mount Olympus, Washington, where the god's
were once rumored to reside, towering
7,980 feet high; and Lewis and Clark Caverns
with a great carved limestone cave, as explorers
they came by; and Arizona's Grand Canyon,

millions of years the Colorado River took to make;
and the Petrified Forest with trees that fell
and fossilized two-hundred million years ago;
and Wyoming's Devil's Tower—a butte
near one mile high that the Great Spirit raised
from the ground below hearing the prayers
of Indian girls in flight from giant bears.
Like a dedicated and tested fire fighter,
you doused the flames of lust of robber
barons who coveted lands that providence
begged to hold in public trust," I said to Theodore
before I pivoted and turned my attention to FDR.
"Franklin, you reassured the country it had nothing
to fear but fear itself in face of Japanese infamy –
a sneak attack hatched within the fog
of shameful, honor-less diplomatic treachery.
You said, enough, America must come to grips
and confront the toxic Nazi ideology and genocidal
racial bigotry that thrust the world into war;
allied and axis powers engaged in bloody battles
that spanned the globe and tested human capacity
to challenge an evil that hell's dark prince unleashed
and fanned with noxious fumes born in hatred's
disaffected soul, a counterfeit currency used
by race-baited radicals to spew the bigot's tarnished,
bogus claim, a fabricated scientific declaration
that spuriously maintained the innate superiority
of one race (white, of course) over all others."
I begged their pardon for my oscillating tendency
and turned once more to Theodore, so together
we might explore how the *Jungle* Sinclair
deplored became his public health emergency.
"Is it truth or fiction Mr. President, that your stomach
turned and you retched when reading Upton's book
exposing slaughter most unsanitary
upon Chicago's sprawling packing floors?"

"Sick enough, I suspect," replied Theodore,
"that I recommended a new law to regulate,
between and among the states, commerce interstate
that trafficked in foods and drugs and drinks.
It's true, I did this for the public's health and safety,
to bar misbranded, debased or altered goods."
"I read in one of my history study-books
that delved in depth into the era historian's
labeled as a progressive time, that you were incensed
by trusts—large, monopolistic businesses –
giant corporations, artificial creatures of the state.
You said with moral force that they must be allegiant
to their sovereign state, and to the judicial courts
where government orders are entrusted to be enforced.
And, now, I'm sad to say the country's highest court
has granted corporations personhood, as if, in fact,
they lived and breathed with fundamental rights attached;
granted rights and status under law the constitution
previously gave only to living citizens,
to breathing people made of flesh and blood,
not printed paper—synthetic and contrived."
The stocky Mr. Roosevelt pursed the drooping mustache
that hid his upper lip, and then his full face turned red
in angry disbelief and uttered, "does no one
feel the misery of this misbegotten tragedy?
What has taken hold and shaken
to its deepest core my beloved country?"
I hesitated for a moment, then plunged ahead,
and said "there's more to share if you wish
for me to expose the gravity of our democracy
as it is now grievously imperiled."
Then like a grizzly mother rising up to roar
in defense of cubs too young to stop a pack
of hungry wolves from sinking teeth in flesh,
the burly one, no teddy bear himself, said "oh God,
let's charge up San Juan Hill once more."

"In nineteen hundred six," I pushed on,
"you pointed to a poisoned press, and called out
William Randolph Hearst and the dangers
of the news contrived, that filled the lines,
the columns, and the pages in his magazines
and newspapers; yellow journalism, lies
personified and twisted truths sensationalized,
that you condemned as a dark and evil force,
an inflammatory influence on the public's discourse,
a blight upon the country's social life and soul."
"That's right, Hearst's news empire had tentacles
everywhere; no home was safe from poisoning.
Hearst was the crafty fox placed cleverly inside
the chicken's coop, spreading lies, fomenting
discord, distrust and fear," responded Theodore.
"It's what today, I and many others condemn as false.
Fake news from the far out right flows now,
like blood through arteries and veins, it
prejudices the public discourse through platforms
so prolific, the populace can hardly comprehend
how its boisterous drones malign and drown out
the endangered, free and centered press."
I sadly nodded to my new-found friend,
before I turned toward his distant cousin
seated in the wheelchair he rode into the room.
"Sir, we have too little time for us to talk
much more of that terrible world war," I said
to the man, the president, the country
and the press referred to and knew as FDR.
"But let me say once more before we close
that door: a plague upon humanity, a curse
upon the human race, was stopped, it's true;
but not before one of history's most heinous ghouls
slaughtered innocent millions after millions
in German slaughter house machines, while
butchers of his villainous regime burned bodies

of the dead they murdered so systematically."
"Please, I'm no longer president, just say Franklin,
if you will. But you are right that was a time
of darkest infamy and woe." I cringed, then said
to FDR, "that unfolded on the world stage,
but let's talk about the struggles here at home,
where you waged another war, a crusade to ease
the plight of human suffering, in a time
of misery, grief and anguished deep despair;
a time when so many, the teaming masses
of our country, had no resources to endure
catastrophic tragedy as unregulated markets
crashed, factories closed, work was lost,
and hunger ruled the day and sleepless nights
within a great depression's crushing grasp."
Franklin placed his hand upon my own, and quietly
spoke to me, "much has been written about the tragedy
of war, but I am most proud, if I can humbly say,
of the Act of Congress that created Social Security."
"Wasn't that," I asked FDR, "part of the better deal,
a New Deal that you proposed for those
who by appearance may seem but ordinary
men perplexed in the extreme of fortunes
misadventure, a populace endangered while
barbarians gathered at the city gates,
the struggling masses who Woody Guthrie
sang of in his album, *The Dust Bowl Ballads*
and his fabled song that touched us all,
This Land is Your Land, if that truth
can still stand the onslaught of oligarchy.
They were the same underrepresented community
who found a champion in a folk-hero of the depression.
William "Will" Rodgers - part Cherokee,
full-time humorist, social commentator,
newspaper columnist writer, screen and stage
entertainer - a hero whose folksy, satire

was captured for posterity in the truth serum
of his prescient humor that he did not make jokes,
he merely observed the practices of governments
and then merely reported the facts he witnessed.
He was a truth-sayer who died, too early drawn
to death, Crowfoot surely would have said.
FDR smiled for a moment, then turned serious
again, in silent acknowledgement of his hour
to act in honor, while mortality sill mattered.
"I only did the decent thing, I did no more
than what a president must do; look out, be about
the policies and programs that address the just pleas
for help from people less fortunate than you."
"Oh, more, so much more my friend," I interrupted FDR.
"It's fair to say you ushered in a twentieth century
American renaissance, a great revival of confidence
and pride, inspiring a renewed spirit of economic security,
and bringing to its end an era of civic and cultural malaise."
Now I was on a roll and hardly could be contained.
"When one in four was unemployed, you turned
to public works, deploying an army of citizens
desperate for work to build new roads and bridges,
dams and airports, hospitals, schools and libraries
for the public good, and built the crucial infrastructure
to mobilize our country's delayed but necessary
response when genocide and destruction came
calling in the specter of the second world war.
You cleaned up the mess the market left
from its crash to Wall Street's corrupted floor,
and set straight the crooked banks, the den of thieves
that closed their doors, blocking trusting customers
from their lost accounts. You, with the courts, turned
around a predatory, unscrupulous industry
until in two thousand seven, in legislative fits
of anti-regulation policies, we again felt
the bitter turn of purchased change as banks

and markets fell precipitously and nearly crashed,
smashed again on a dirty brokered floor."
"Still, as far as I am concerned, I hope historians
accurately reflect in charity that forgives
my other sins," replied Franklin Roosevelt,
"that it was the Social Security Act that crowned
my presidency, and gave to posterity a safety net
for individuals to avoid the fretful plunge
deep into poverty's abyss, and helped families
in real need from being torn apart, from blowing
apart in the dusty winds of chance and the heartless
cruelty of naturally occurring chaotic happenstance."
I nodded to the man seated in his metal chair,
and said with all the passion I could summon:
"a legacy of supplementary pensions for the aged,
insurance for the temporary unemployed,
essential aid and health care benefits
for needy children and the disabled,
is without question a noble testament
to your determined will to make the lives
of common men and women better
because of government exercise."
Both men, the two Roosevelts and I,
shared a glance and then, without a sound,
puff, they disappeared; vanished, gone again,
missing from the room, presumably, like
the other transitory visitors fleeing from my dream.
Then more came, unacknowledged, no hush,
no open mouths, no wide-eyed stares
from those within the room, as the new arrivals
walked humbly through my dream's
peculiar portal door. One young women,
her head covered in a scarf, preceded
three older men, all of whom had been nominated
for the Noble Prize, and all but one - an elderly man
from India - had been bestowed peace' most honored

accolade. A Hindu, a Muslim, and two Christians, too.
Three had past and one still lived, surviving
a zealot's vicious act of unadulterated hate,
censorship in its most heightened state.
But for two of them fate had sadly intervened,
as bullets from a rifle and a hand-held gun
killed them dead before their natural time;
and death, although a necessary end,
came calling prematurely as cruel fate
did not spare the slaughter of these saints.
Gandhi, King, Mandela, and Yousafzai; saints,
if ever blessed saints walked upon this earth.
They shared a common thread as people
disadvantaged, separated not by God
and heaven's hosts but spun on the hooved
beast's spinning wheel of hate segregated
rigidly into prejudicial castes and discriminating
racial categories, by those with the power
to do men ill who describe so many sisters
and brothers of the human race subordinate,
inferior in their twisted minds to their imagined,
fabricated superior Aryan white.
Malala, in a kindly show of reverence, asked Bapu,
the venerable, respectfully to pass in front of her,
as they moved in close to greet and meet with me.
I marveled at the honor I received, that four
great souls such as these would grace their saintly
presence upon a common man like me, as I felt
my wife and children's loving hands gently grasp
my hands and stroke my arms and cheek.
Gandhi wore a hand spun shawl and woven cloth
which wrapped around his waist and legs,
snugged with a knot mid-waist above the hips.
He pressed his palms together inches from his chest
and bowed his head ever slightly, his Hindi Mudra's
greeting meaning "I salute you," given in respect

to honor his encounter with another living human being.
Malala interjected, "Bapu, means papa and father, too."
I smiled warmly and asked Gandhi, "may I
call you papa or do you prefer Bapu?"
"Either one, my kind friend, is equally fine
with me," Gandhi replied quietly.
"So, how on earth did you succeed,
when in failure all others seemed to fall,
while you dethroned Great Britain's
once invincible, imperial rule?
No military force before could bring
to your beloved India self-determination,
and independence with inherent rights
attached," I asked the venerated holy man
who gave no more than all himself to garner
my high esteem and affectionate regard.
"It was a matter of resolve; a firm, determined,
unrepentant, unrelenting, defiant 'No'
that altered the apparent will of gods and kings,
and righteousness, of course, that rolled
on like angry waves across a troubled sea.
We stood against the overreach of British
tax on salt, as your countrymen, in rebellion,
once did the same regarding English taxes
they exacted, unfairly placed on tea."
"We did this peacefully," his hallow face
nodding solemnly, and said: "we held the line
like soldiers serving loyally in an army valiantly,
standing side by side, facing down the arrogance
of the proud, who threatened punishments
that despots throughout history have meted
out in savage retributions aimed to bring
to an ignoble end to all that tends to good.
But the strength of civility came hard and fast
like a mythological hero riding on a white stag.
Emboldened in the lawful cause of men

and women singing freedom's song, willful civility
proved to be a stronger moral force dejure
in the long march of freedom to its final end;
upending Britain's mighty occupying force,
vanquished in tears and blood shed peacefully,
a prime defense and counterpoint to a vaunted
war machine's weapons of suppression,
and oppression, destruction and death."
"And so, one star died that another might
be born," I said with a sense of justice
too long denied, with the knowledge
that something new had just arrived.
"You lived a simple life, a diet free of meat,
and frequent fasting. But was it true as rumored
some fasts you threatened, if justice was not served,
you would hold the fast until your death."
"That's only partially true," Bapu replied to me.
"I fasted to protest religious hate and bigotry
between Muslim Pakistan and Hindu India.
Turbulence filled the air when the world' ruling
powers, believing condescendingly, they knew
best for us, divided India into separate countries.
When independence came at last, a new India
and Pakistan were thrust upon the world stage,
a new sovereign north and south historical divide,
indifferent to the complex math leaving each
with populations out of place; minorities displaced,
ripe for persecution's ugly curse, abandoned, trapped
within new drawn borders upon an arbitrary map,
a contorted globe presenting an open invitation
to homicide and large-scale genocide.
But not all the fasting was political,
there was another side; for fasting,
working like the ocean's tides, can also
be an enlightened conscious exercise
for purging dangerous toxins from the body

and sparking from within a spiritual renewal.
Some decried, condemned me as an old
accommodating fool, as I condemned, without
regard of cult and geography, castaways outside
redemption's veil who justified impiously
in the name of their god divine, hatred, murder,
and religious genocide in bloody wars of senseless
human sacrifice to the triumph of their gods
whom they believed supreme," Bapu replied to me.
My eyes swelled with tears no dam could hold back,
"and your high-souled nobility led a Hindu devotee,
drawn from among a legion of fanatic malcontents
to steal away your precious life from you.
Your life he took, but your honor stayed
defiantly, subverting his cruel act to take away
time not fully measured out for you."
"To forfeit your life in defense of moral right
and social justice must never be a cost too high
to pay. Besides," Bapu said, his lips curving
upward tenderly, "I was quite old, and weary
from battles lost and won, and in fate's mercy
never had to suffer age's final cruel decay."
I said to him, "I have read the prose and poetry
of Kahlil Gibran and conclude his perspectives
on the efficacy of western religions and their gods
justifies a coroner's inquest and paneled inquiry.
Peace might follow naturally, in spite of territorial
tenacity, if his words were heard and given currency.
Then people could accept the wisdom I found
within his words, and like me hold the messages
close within their hearts and minds. He wrote,
what I would call a sacred Abrahamic text,
that if expanded, without prejudice laid out
upon a universal plane, love would flow
to those who bow, kneel, pray, chant, or meditate;
whenever, wherever, be it in mosques, temples,

churches, shrines, or seated underneath a single tree,
all are seeking insight into divine truth's illusive imagery."
I saw the pained expression on his face as his hands
moved close together near the center of his chest.
Then Bapu, the reverent one, in humble modesty,
bowed ever slightly and said to me, "you're right
to say the poet, you extol, perceived the common
thread among western religions born of Abraham,
and that if expanded universally might usher in
a spring of newfound human love. But, I observe
his words are empty for the primitive indigenous;
for Hindus like myself, Buddhists, Taos, and yes,
too, for those who marvel at nature's majesty
but take the atheist or agnostic view."
He paused for the briefest moment, then smiled
warmly as he said, "the tribal roots that led
to human evolutionary gains are adaptive traits
engineered in early human brains; genetic messages
encoded for survival of our species that still hold sway
and compel humanity down a predatory path
of tribal clans and cults that obsess on differences
dividing us, obscuring from our sight basic interests,
and our elemental, common roots and needs.
But I have hope that others understand the folly
of exclusiveness, and will carry on the righteous
march toward tolerance and inclusiveness.
I admit it will not come easily, but come it will,
if determined humans pass it on in gene pools
that mutate from their ancient roots; changed to see
survival of the self and human kind linked in necessity
to cooperation, collaboration and the common good."
I tried but failed to return a Mudra to the saintly servant
of the common man. I cursed the dream that restrained
my hands, denying me the chance to reciprocate.
I felt my wife's hand brush my falling hair aside,
and with that wisp and gentle motion Bapu,

the venerable, departed from my dream.
Then, within the flicker of a dying candle's flame,
came a Christian man, another saintly soul
appended to my dream; a pastoral man
who spawned a revolution across a troubled land,
a land cursed by a deafened God who could
not hear or feel the sorrow in his people's cries.
He bore witness true to Christ's recorded works
of peace and charity, and in inspiration's art
of imitation adapted Gandhi's proven strategies
of civil resistance to government policies
that support a false religion of inequality.
He was the spearhead of a movement
to end segregation and prejudice based on race,
perpetrated against an entire race of Black Americans
for whom Lincoln's proclamation of emancipation
was turned askew, a hollow, empty, promissory shell,
like treaties with the American Indian tribes,
a piece of paper much ignored, until a revolution
swept across the land; a peaceful one,
but not free of precious human tears and blood.
"You were only twenty-six," I said to Dr. King,
"when you took on old Alabama, a remnant
of the shameful antebellum past, with a boycott
of the public buses that segregated passengers
in scurrilous regulations solely based on race,
in their inherent right to travel freely in the public
buses that traversed Montgomery streets.
And, as a young man, not a novice, but early
in the fight for civil rights, you wrote with moral
force your famous letter from the Birmingham jail.
And then, there was the historic march
on the Great Mall at our nation's capital,
where your voice thundered out the dream
you had, that all God's children—black and white,
the rainbow of humanity—would reach a promised land,

a land of civil rights, of freedom and equality;
a place where sons and daughters of former
slaves and slaveholders might in peace sit down
with God around a table set in brotherhood."
Dr. King, a minister without a cleric's collar,
wore a dark suit, white shirt and tie, neatly dressed
I remarked to my wife, who always said she liked
the way I looked when I would leave for work
in stylish suits, with coordinated shirts and ties,
and a homburg hat in the chill and cold of wintertime.
"Yes, and the dream, the hope, though unrealized
still persists," said Dr. King, his voice, serious,
sonorous, and unflinchingly sincere.
"With help from LBJ, despite our deep divide
on the Asian War America waged in Viet Nam,
we surged ahead with voting rights, as I turned
my attention to remediate the poverty that plagued
the poor, to say a resounding 'No' to the beast
that would beat my people down and grind
their faces on the rocks of poverty. I did this, while
President Johnson pushed his agenda to close
the open door, to clear out the stubborn vestiges
of antebellum prejudices and racial inequality,
and to redress, reform, and lift off the heavy weight
of poverty, to stem the greed that works so hard
to hold impoverished eyelids down, an outrageous
hypocrisy in this land of good and plenty."
"His Great Society," I replied, "Lyndon Johnson's
legacy though clouded by that damn unnecessary
war is one that I can say is worthy of our praise.
Although John and Robert Kennedy called out
for social justice, the task of moving intent to action
and accomplishment fell to a southerner, a Stetson
hatted Texas cattle rancher who twisted and cajoled
political allies and enemies alike, and channeled
massive federal funds to legislative programs

advancing public education, health and medicine,
and curbing urban problems and rural poverty.
On his watch, came Medicare and Medicaid,
and aid to older Americans, and new safety nets
unmatched since Franklin Roosevelt's transforming
Social Security Insurance Act and America's New Deal."
I smiled for a moment while Dr. King just looked
quizzically at me, as I said as a proud Ohioan,
"he first coined the phrase 'the Great Society'
at a speech in Athens on the college campus
of Ohio University, the alma mater of my son."
Then I digressed and allowed myself a moment
of boastfulness: "I once was a Council's chief executive,
working with a board of public university presidents.
We worked together to advance higher education,
its public interests, purposes, and its crucial contributions
to science, medicine, social justice, economic development,
and educational opportunity, all aimed with commitment
toward the common good and society's betterment."
"Please call me by my given name, it was my fathers, too;
I much prefer Martin with my friends, and I now count
you one of them," said the Reverend Doctor King
as he reached out and clasped my hand in his.
"Now tell me of how things have gone astray."
"Oh, where to start," I began. "Egypt's locust plagues
in frightful biblical display seems trivial to the *ists, isms*
and *phobes* that afflict our country's endangered soul."
"So, let me move to the twisted tale of the tape
of the savage fight - a holy war, if war itself could
lay such claim - that might determine, perhaps
not once and for all, but for now, until
some great reforming renaissance can reclaim
homo sapiens' imperiled ego-centric claim
that it is earth's ultimate evolutionary game."
"Don't pull your punches," Martin said to me.
"Speak the truth no matter how hard the blows rain

their savage black and blue bruising truth down on me."
"Lyndon Johnson's gone, and despite the fact we had an
African-American president, the great society, the shining
city on the hill, is being pushed by monsters, sliding
headlong to an inglorious death, consumed in a sea
of molten anger stoked by old hates renewed."
"What did you mean by *ists, isms* and *phobes*,"
Dr. King asked earnestly of me. "'It's a hard truth
but it must be told,'" I said in pained solemnity.
"There is a new trail of tears that in my nightmares
I have traveled through, populated with outlaws
tearing at the rule of law; an army of narcissists,
nationalists and would be fascists, anti-immigrant racists,
bigots, white-supremist homophobes and xenophobes.
Now hordes of bleating sheep, oblivious and unaware,
march blindly to a false prophet's piper tune;
entranced, deceived, they lurch in blindness
to what they think will be their good fortune.
But only misfortune looms, as the gullible are led
toward a crimson slaughter house floor wherein
they, too, will be sacrificed to satisfy the lust
and the unmitigated greed of the one percent;
America's parallel to the Russian mafia, the rapacious
wealthy class - our own obscene, insatiable oligarchs;
a despotism John Adams warned of in a letter
written to Thomas Jefferson far back in 1815.
This is America's new ruling class. It hoards its wealth
secured from loyal commoners; paupers snared
in the midst of enormous wealth that is bonded
in unethical purchases of policies' that history
will condemn as fraudulent and criminal; a prelude
to the worst of times, cataclysmic in its aftermath
for the 99 percent trapped outside the gaudy palaces
with golden toilets for the foul poop of the covetous."
I saw the tears, and sensed the pain
that brought them to his eyes, and felt

their moisture falling and reach my hand,
looked up and Dr. King had quickly taken leave,
putting pain and disbelief aside, while I
in abject sadness tried my best to cry,
but could not summon tears that once
flowed easily for movies, plays and books,
and so much more for history's callous, cruel,
and heinous acts, and villainous autocrat's
guilt for crimes against humanity.
Vapors vanish in the air, like the great souls
passing through the dreams that occupy my mind
in night sleep's turbulence; as one focus fades
and another stream of thoughts are born
in the stubborn triumph of the subconscious mind
and its mysterious dominance of our receptive brains.
I met his eyes emerging from the fog of dreams,
a deep and penetrating gaze awakened me
from the momentary gap - the twist and switch
so ordinary in the machinations of my restless sleep.
He grasped my resting hand with a brother's care,
while I felt the cold, coiled steel his grip belied.
I was certain that a force of nature coursed beneath
the surface of this complex and complicated man.
"Mr. Mandala," I exclaimed, as I recognized yet another
architect of revolutionary change, a late acknowledged
winner of a noble prize of peace—one man among
a host of mother Africa's colony of army ants,
freedom fighters who with blood and tears,
and a mighty effort of relentlessly determined will,
upended South Africa's sesquipedalian, suffocating,
segregationist swill, and ushered in a new era—
a time of refuge in confession with admission
to an ugly past. And this, was accomplished without
revenge, through a simultaneous reconciliation based
on fact, not forgetting antecedent sins and crimes
but moving on to emancipation; guilt admitted

with mercy reconciled as blacks and whites
were freed from the shackles and the pain
of human suffering born of insidious apartheid.
That is the mortal sin white supremist South Africans
will for centuries hence carry like the heavy chain
that Dickens' Mr. Scrooge greedy, selfish friend,
poor Marley in his ghostly sad reflective dream.
"You, like our former President, Mr. Obama, were a first,
the first man of color to be your country's Head of State.
You were lawfully elected leaders elevated by the votes
of free people, people whom the power brokers, long
the arbiters of outcomes literally guaranteed, sought
to suppress and treacherously to impede
the cobbled path of freedom and of liberty
while their crimes, unlike the French, escaped
the sharp fate of an avenging guillotine.
Knowledge is the only weapon that can arrest
these brazen public felons who attempt through laws
crafted purposefully to obstruct and deny
the populace lawful opportunities to exercise
the voting rights that natural law bequeaths to all."
I paused for a moment, my searching mind stuck
on how to frame the question I was pained to ask;
I had to ask this honored man who helped lead
his kinsmen's bloody struggle in a war of danger
and intrigue, and insurrection aimed to end
South Africa's race-conscious, odious apartheid.
For his alleged transgressions, he was sent
to prison for inciting terror and other criminal
misdeeds that his captors touted white-powered
claims of treason and treachery, ferried him away
like Edmund Dantes to his island of Chateau d'If;
ocean current captive Robben Island Prison complex.
There, for eighteen of the twenty-seven years
he spent imprisoned; his freedom forfeit,
his captors hoped until death doomed his soul.

He was sacrificed as others in freedom's march,
like lambs tethered waiting to be slaughtered
in tribute to the devil-god of white supremacy.
"How is it that a gentle soul like you vacillated
back and forth, deploying first the political ideals
of Gandhi and then of Dr. King, and their use
of nonviolent civil disobedience and peaceful protests
for civil rights in their indomitable separate quests
for independence and equality? Then later,
faced with a seemingly impenetrable wall
of white intransigency, reversed your course
and acquiesced to the use of violent tactics, means
John Brown and Nat Turner once used in fighting
slavery in the USA" I asked him pensively.
"No one goes unblemished fighting hellish fiends
and the corrupt practices they impose on tortured
souls," he replied without hesitation or remorse.
"I exhausted all means my people could accommodate.
I saw no other choice and I regressed. I closed my eyes
to violence, course and gross, forcing reluctant men
on both sides finally to negotiate face to face
in honest brokered trust and good faith.
Only then," he said, his voice rasping in bitter irony,
"could we pivot back to a peaceful path, forge ahead,
make real progress, and avoid a bloody war of race
the world could not, would not, long endure."
He said, "this was the right path, the only passage
we discerned to make it through Galileo's dark labyrinth.
It was a hard and pock marked path with tense
negotiations, navigating through a harsh climate
otherwise completely indisposed, odorant
to meaningful political compromise.
We found our elusive solution, ultimately,
in a reconciliation process that granted absolution
to transgressors who acknowledged culpability
and confessed in public to their crimes.

I knew no other way to slay the deadly dragon.
I did not see another way to kill the beast that would
otherwise destroy the vestiges of imperiled humanity
still enslaved inside my country's desperate soul,
that I, or no savior of my race, could much longer pacify."
He stood still and silent for a second, hardly more,
before he turned toward the waiting door, just as
Ms. Malala Yousafzai moved in view along my side.
So young, I reflected to myself; a noble prize, and she,
at least by half, the youngest of the four sword-less
samurais; warriors advancing in fearless protest
to wage holy war against the politics of inequality.
Oh, I was grateful for my dream's meandering course
and for the opportunity to speak with this brave, heroic
woman; a young Pakistani girl who dared to challenge
repressive men within the Taliban who barred girls
from attending school, bent on keeping women
uneducated, suppressed, forever victims violated
in a misogyny that was culturally congealed.
I knew her story well but asked the question anyway:
"you were shot by a gunman from the Taliban
for advocating decency with human rights
and education for girls in your native Pakistan?"
"Mercifully, I did not die from the wound inflicted
in a Fattah's retaliation for speaking out for girls
like myself, that we might be viewed with dignity,
and have rights and opportunities that males
in our rooted culture have long had access to,"
was her forthright, pained, high-spirited response.
"You, among your traveling peers, are the only one alive,"
I said. "And women everywhere need your advocacy:
for girls in Pakistan who long for education and equal
rights with men, and in other Muslim lands where women
have no voting rights and privileges of employment,
and where driving licenses are denied. And yes,
in my country too, where men would rule the day,

and have the final say over women's souls
at their deepest core, saying women lack the basic
human right to make their own decisions regarding
the care and health of themselves."
Our eyes in mourning met, as I continued on:
"there is more tragedy here than anyone with open eyes
can see, as history tells a tale that women in my country
who have historically been suppressed and once
held no rights to property, no right to vote, no
route to hold public office, or to work for pay equal
in measure to wages paid to their male counterparts.
And now, we have leaders, called out for misogyny, one
in claims made credible through sheer numbers of complaints
against a man who once bragged brazenly and openly,
in a recorded interview, how he viewed women as objects
to exploit, not as precious human beings, but servile pawns
to satisfy the appetite of his aggrandized self."
I saw the tears swell in her eyes, and said compassionately,
"and while his sycophant supporters deprecate Muslims
as a global threat, Christian, evangelical fundamentalists,
urged on by charlatan profiteering ministers of hate,
turn blind eyes toward the damning facts, the mountain
of compelling evidence substantiating the misogyny,
bigotry, hatred, and dangerous poison toxins
of xenophobes and homophobes, and their specious
claims of religious and racial inferiority; claims
that have emboldened and unleashed the Baskerville
fiends of a prejudicial hell, and spreads a cloudy mist
that drags our tarnished country inexorably toward
the deadly bogs of internal discord and decay."
Once again, I felt the moisture of a salty human tear
drop onto my hand, the one that still held within its fingers
Crowfoot's eagle feather; then looked up and brave, heroic
Malala was gone, escaping from my dream, moving on,
I presumed, to fight with all the passion in a saintly martyr's
precious life for justice, charity, compassion and equality

for women, and by extrapolation, for all humanity
unencumbered access to basic education and health care,
clean water and clean air, the bounty of the earth's
waiting harvests, and all humankind for fundamental rights,
attendant, inherent and unalienable, sustaining human life.
I was instantly aware; his presence unmistakable,
unless, of course, you were afflicted with
the Aryan supremacy disease that left no quarter,
no place to contemplate, no scientific counter point
to blind belief in an anglicized White Christ.
He steadily advanced across the room, Jesus,
the Christ, the Son of God, incarnate in earthly
mortal flesh. I could not see, but felt the heat,
the magnetic aura surrounding him as he
moved ever closer to my awaiting side.
Some allege that he is enveloped by a halo
of bright light, but that must be their imaginations
in extreme, for I truly did not see a girding light,
but I do admit who can say with any certainty,
what a dog standing by its master's side sees,
hears and smells a thousand yards away, far beyond
the range my eyes, and ears and nose can sense.
Does the dog sense more than me? Does the canine
apprehend something more than cold, stark, natural
reality, something just beyond the thin veil separating
life and death, or is it merely a distant cousin, Canis
lupus, a primal wolf on a surreptitious prowl?
His skin was brown and weathered, exposed;
heated in the sun, chafed by the wind,
and rubbed rough by abrasive desert sand.
His features were not Aryan, for he was born
of ancient, nomadic, tribal clans forged on the anvil
arching east across North Africa through Arabia's
Peninsula that slides past 21st century pirates prowling
off the coastal shores of Somali out to the open sea.
His hair was black, shoulder length, with tangles

that curled naturally. His eyes, a common Aramaic brown,
had speckles the moon could illuminate in the nighttime sky;
eyes that when struck by the daytime sun's intrusive light
danced across the lens that opened wide a portal
to his wounded, martyred holy soul.
His arms and legs, protruding out beyond
the sleeves and bottom of his tattered robe,
where thin with muscles resembling twisted strands
of rope; evidence that his arms were not strangers
to a day laborer's tasks, and his calves carved out
of marble stone rivaled marching centurions'
well-traveled, cadenced, booted feet and legs.
I was nearly in a state of ecstasy, euphoric and aflame,
a giddy child exuberant in a deferred expectancy
that I hardly could contain—a rain filled cloud
about to burst and drench the thirsting ground below.
For, I was soon, so long delayed, prepared
to consummate a lifetime of pursuit, the hunter's
haunting desperate quest to find its most elusive prey.
I was, I thought excitedly, armed and ready to confront,
or better yet, to converse with this man generations
have called the Son of God; the unrelenting beast
who forced himself upon my subconsciousness,
in frightful dreams that scarily tormented me, and
teased and stoked the doubts that plagued my fretful
timid mind to a point of caustic cynical distain.
I asked him straight out and quite impulsively,
"You are the Jesus written of in Qumran cave scrolls
and ancient sacred texts that Mark and Mathew,
Luke and John entranced in a shaman's hallucinating
glimpse wrote the news they called "Good"
in languages, not your Aramaic own, that now
inspire and enmesh a billion modern followers
who call upon you as their living God, no more
a humble carpenter, a simple, struggling man."
"Never, not once," he was quick to say,

"did I ever say I had a stake, a claim to divinity.
I was, like you and every other living human being,
a simple son of man—no holy spirit traveling
from another realm; nothing extraordinaire;
just an ordinary common man, a working carpenter."
"But what . . . ," he cut me off before I could ask
the questions, I had placed like arrows in a leather
quiver, to pierce the books of Mark and Mathew,
Luke and John. "They are myths, those books;
full of recast metaphors and allegories, garish
embellishments made by men who heard
the lesson-laden stories handed down a hundred times
and more, with each story-teller trying hard to add
spice and salt and pepper to the magic of the tales."
His gaze, when set, was mesmerizing; juxtaposed
in odd alignment with a voice that soothed and
conveyed a gentle, rhythmic, reassuring tone.
"It was John, my younger brother, not the gospel
author John, who was the first to make the quantum
leap, the jump across the great abyss, to claim
that I was somehow divine, profound and different
from the ordinary cut of man. Now, different,
I will concede, but divine was much too far a hurdle,
unless you mean that all men are divine –
the seeing, hearing, smelling, tasting, touching ones
who give life and shape to God; one and all,
sons and daughters of the great creative surge,
the burst of life infusing brilliant light," he remarked
softly like a gentle, loving master giving tender
finger strokes underneath the fury muzzle of
his faithful spotted-shepherd herding dog.
"It was not me," he said emphatically, "it was the
'good news' gospel quartet and that prolific letter writing
Paul, who borrowed Greek and Roman mythology
and misapplied their godly qualities to things I did
and said." He shrugged his shoulders and shook

his disheveled head, and conveying disbelief,
drew in a deep breath, exhaled a somber sigh,
then said: "a virgin birth, the roots of that are traced
to Greek and Roman mythology, a tautology absent
from, an affront to my native Hebrew creed.
Jehovah did not from heaven come to mount
my mother in her dreams. I was born to Mary
and to Joseph, conceived on their wedding bed;
a first-born son, their child, a son of man,
most assuredly not the sole son of God."
You see," he said, "the writers made miraculous,
amplified a thousand times, the ordinary circumstances
my words detailed, and actions may have exemplified."
"I confess to you, I have since puberty been skeptical
of the miracle traditions," I said, sincerely, not shy or
timid, staring bravely at my amazing guest –
a visitor who no longer resembled the haunting,
savage, unrelenting warrior beast that slayed
my nighttime sleep. "I must say," I said steadfastly,
"I never could understand how water came to wine;
how you cured the sick by merely laying on your hands;
how a small cache of fish and bread could feed a throng
of people crowded close at hand to hear a sermon
from a disaffected revolutionary, a free style teaching
thinker who the religious elders greatly feared
and universally despised; and most of all, how a man
was crucified, died a gruesome, horrifying death,
was buried in a tomb nearby, and then somehow
was resurrected, cheating death, denying Charon's
haunting, dreaded one-way trip to death."
"I am pleased, my traveling friend, that we have time
to talk and perhaps to give your thirsting, searching mind
some answers to your soul's unquenchable quest,
its endless search for the golden fleece, the chalice
of the holy grail, the path up the mountain to Olympus peak,"
said the humble Jesus as he grasped my hand lovingly.

"Let me tell you of the wedding feast in Cana of Galilee,
where the writer John claimed the miracle of changing
water into wine," Jesus said, as a circumscribing smile
surfaced on the contours of his benevolent face.
"It is true, my mother came to me and said the host
was out of wine and asked if there anything I could do
to help this man in need, who had generously
invited our entire family to his daughter's wedding feast.
So, where is the choice, when a mother asks a son
to do what he can to help a friend?
I had met a vineyard owner at the feast, who
in conversation said his vines were in distress
and needed water soon. It's a gift I thought;
a solution was at hand, as we had recently
drawn six large urns of water for my shop,
and so, an exchange was quickly arranged.
The vineyard owner's servants took our water
hurriedly to the thirsty vines, returned in haste,
the empty water urns then filled with vineyard wine.
And that, my friend, was what that crafty author
John fashioned as the miracle of water into wine."
I nodded in acknowledgement, then asked
Christ, Jesus, "what of feeding thousands
in a crowd with an insignificant cache of fish
and a single bag of flat round loaves of bread?"
He squeezed my hand and said so casually,
"that was Mathew skillfully blending one story
into two: separating the catch of fish and distribution
of loaves of bread from the sermon on the sloping hill
that overlooked the nearby river shore.
The crowd was small that gathered near
and I asked the fishermen Peter and his crew
who followed us about, to share their daily catch,
to trade some fish for the baker's bread
that we might ease the hunger of the small
assembled crowd, several dozen at best,

not multitudes, that had come to hear me speak.
And, while Mathew's account told a tale
of a fabled sermon on the mount, he made
much more of it than actually transpired.
My message was hardly new or trending
to sublime: I said that God requires action
on our part, and peace of mind comes only
to those who show mercy and magnanimity;
not wait for God, wherever he might in hiding be,
in his own time, in small measures met it out.
We earn no wage or praise unless we work
and labor tirelessly for a world buoyed
with tranquility and for a long enduring peace
between and among mankind. I said that no one
should be a stranger to our house; the sick, the poor,
the troubled and distressed, men and women equally,
and loving couples and partners caught out beyond
convention's laws, all are precious fellow human
travelers whose presence grace our lives. All these,
and more, we should welcome in our homes.
I came, I said, to reject a life withdrawn, secluded,
cult-like, and that it was a selfish act to escape
and to withdraw, immersed within ourselves.
I came to cast aside the old conventions
in our Covenant, to smash the old and usher
in the new; a testament, a new Covenant
with God that eschews retribution and revenge,
and calls on men and women, the impoverished
and the powerful, the familiar and the strange,
to grace the earth with charity and compassion,
to forgive others and ourselves for failings, insults
and slights. I came, it's true, to free humanity,
to extricate women and men from a cruel
exacting God and his obsolete worn out
old testament for life. I said, and meant,
there was no sin in love, or food or wine,

unless it turned unfaithfully, or fell disgracefully
into gluttony and drunkenness."
Tears welled within his haunting eyes and trickled
down his sunburned cheeks as he poured out
the disappointment in his heart for women's plight;
a piercing, disparaging affront, a glaring lack
of fundamental rights and equality within the rule
of law was his condemnatory cry: "No day passes
where I do not shout out to God on high,
that women are afflicted still by prejudice,
transgressed, abused by practices misogynist
and injurious to a new testament's behavior guides.
The devil claps its hands in glee as ministers of God,
and the sheep that follow like a bleating herd
fleeing from a hungry predator, tell women
they have no right, no power to decide, to choose,
much less control the sacred body God has bestowed
on them equally with men. Two thousand years
I have wept, and filled an ocean full of salty tears,
while men see women no different than potter's urns
filled with water or with wine, or beasts of burden
that must endure and carry on full term, like a camel
captive in a meandering destitute desert caravan.
It's women, not men," he said vehemently,
"who should decide what course a pregnancy
should take. If the cause is found in incest, rape,
or a girl is taken underage, or imminent risk
or death to the women is likely to obtain,
then a loving God in heaven cannot condemn
women's pained, soulful reasoned choice.
I find it difficult to grasp that men and women
followers of a conservative Christian right,
evangelical devotees who readily accept
the premise life ends when we take our last
gasping breath cannot apprehend that life begins
when the unborn draws its first breath, or at least

in modern times not before a fetus floating like a fish
with gills in the birthing ooze breathes independently
in the earthly air outside its mother's womb."
I sensed the coming of a storm; a volcanic gush
of anger that would shake hell to its burnt core
erupting in an all-consuming flame, sparing Troy
a second fire and releasing all the lost souls
whom God dispelled, trapped within walls of hell.
"Oh, there is hypocrisy afoot in reasoning
where people ardently shout out 'we are pro-life'
but only hold that course until some poor infant
draws a breath, and then turn their backs
and abandon it; rejecting taxes and tithes
that support the best that any government
can do to strive in earnest in its policies and laws
to render unto its populace a route to happiness
through programs aimed to end a family's hunger,
promote a child's health, its safety and its education,
and stakes out a decent chance for it to find joy,
and secure a fair head-start toward success in life.
They're fools, those cold, uncaring selfish ones,
who think that a child can support itself,
oblivious to a parent's circumstance."
I felt his pain. I shared the depth of his chagrin,
but I could not relent or give up quite yet
as other primal questions begged answers
I had no luxury or time remaining to delay.
"And the stories of your miraculous healing powers
that brought cures for afflictions and from disease,
are they too fabrications drafted by the men who wrote
the good news books," I asked incredulously.
"No, my friend," the humble man said patiently,
"some are false but, there are small kernels
of the truth clinging to that battered ear of corn.
I could not heal a leper from his dread disease,
or cause the lame to walk, and certainly

not raise the dead to life again, but
the writer Mark was closest to the truth.
I was a teacher of a sort, a counselor if you will
concede. My lesson in its essence was simplicity,
but not a simple truth; life is best if we strive
to be less harsh on others and ourselves.
Some might prefer to say I was more like
a modern therapist who could help a person
with a troubled mind find a way to navigate
a path they could traverse, that they might
gain freedom from their psychological malaise.
As a teacher I did not seek to affect eternity.
I only sought to give receptive souls hope
for them in the sacred moment of a single day."
"And the crucifixion," I asked tentatively,
"wherein is the truth in that divine mystery?"
"The pretext was important, but no more
then than now," he solemnly replied.
"Don't cry for me, my friend, for restful death
delayed was not my fate to be. The priestly
and the privileged classes conspired, as they often
do, to pervert the ruling legal system to enforce
their self-serving religious codes. It is an evil incarnate,
an unholy alliance that rains down its toxic
volcanic ash on the just and unjust alike.
I am convinced this was the reason
why the gathered crowd, its well-positioned
mob placed within, was bated by the priests
and power class, and in self-interest called out
'give us Barabbas' when Pontius Pilate asked
who should be pardoned, who should be released,
who would not face, and who would secure release
from the demon curse of crucifixion's cross."
Our eyes were locked, not the slightest chance
that he or I would blink, or voluntarily
turn away from each other's piercing gaze,

as we peered into the molten center
of the very essence of our kindred souls.
"Your teacher friend, your beloved Nikos
I am afraid had this one point wrong,"
he said sympathetically. "I did not seek
to die, or for my death to save humanity.
I never saw that as a purposed path.
That is a myth encoded in the hero story cult,
portrayed in caves where Neanderthals once dwelt,
that helped humans cope and rationalize
the anguish they endure, as they grappled
like wary sailors tossed about on a callous,
unforgiving sea with the painful separation
that sails with us attendant to our deaths.
The meaning of the parable that heaven
was close at hand is greatly misconstrued.
I did not mean that some men and women
among the crowd would not die before heaven
opened its gilded gates and ushered in a golden era
restoring David's glorious reign," said Jesus,
as he shook his bearded head in genuine chagrin.
"They misapplied the message, they could not
in the dawning of a new day let go of past regrets
for future fears of what lies ahead. The parable
was intended exclusively to point out that heaven
is at hand; it is the Now. We make our heaven
or our hell in the acts and the silence of omissions
that define the contours and the shape of each
gifted day we have to live or waste; a gift
from our creator whomever that might be, who seeks
adoration for the gift we have received,
not narcissistic praise bestowed upon himself.
It was clear to me that heaven is a single day,
a thin slice in time when I find my way to see,
hear, speak and touch others, and seek to understand
my inner self, and do so with compassion, charity

and without conditions holding back my love."
I saw his trembling hand and heard anger rising
in his voice as he said emphatically, "I was a father
and a husband, a son and a brother. I was loved
and I loved others too, and never sought an early exit
to enter heaven's gate, to flee from this gifted
life to lapse ignobly into eternity. I never said
I was a god divine, not once! I knew deep within
there is no return from death, no resurrection
for the crucified, no place to carry on the endless quest,
no land where our spirits endure and eternally reside;
that truth is missing in the 'good news' manuscripts.
I was not the Jewish Messiah, foretold by prophets
of a savage, patriarchal, desert-roaming, tribal faith,"
he said with calculated measured emphasis,
and then went on to say: "There is a question
so obvious, that it must be asked; how could
a caring human being tolerate the creeping pace
of such a selfish, petty god? Where is the grandeur
of a god that hides from rank offense and
finds its cursed, elusive peace in sacrificing the child,
it has sired, in a twisted, tragic abuse of love;
a deviant act that its apologists incongruously
proclaim is the only route this rigid God could
contemplate to forgive the very image of itself.
Where is the sin original for invention's natural
evolutionary urge to seek out knowledge, to taste
the flavor seared within the eternal intellectual quest,
to find an answer to creation's great conundrum,
to discover the river's source, and to obtain a clear
understanding of the confounding dreaded cycle
that circles life and death?" He challenged me,
"where is the mortal sin in this, that man dares
eat from the fruit of a tree that brings insight
and the knowledge to see and sense the presence
of the great creative surge from which we

and all that ever was, is, and will be, emerge,
including God itself with whom we are one?"
He stayed for a moment more and then said,
"I'm glad and positively relieved we had
this splendid opportunity. I hope it helps
to bring you peace as it has done for me.
'It is done' those are the words I cried out
as I took my last gasping breath, and so,
it is for us my friend; it is done, and now again,
I must take my leave," he said, released
my hand from his, whispered in my ear
'shalom aleikhem' and vanished from my sight,
another actor exiting the stage from a final scene.
It's an abstraction, the paintings of the madcap
artist of our wildest dreams, or the words penned
by a manic writer who howls in pain openly
to a pale blue moon that only he can see,
a struggling author who confounds us with perplexing
incongruencies. We are left troubled, sad and quite mad
that neither artist or the author offers tidy explanations
that chronicle logically the mysteries hidden deep
within the subterranean folds of our subconsciousness –
the seething, volcanic magna of the caldera of our minds.
So, why would the Buddha not be seated by my side
in a leather reclining chair, resting peacefully
with his feet crossed and hands folded in his lap?
That was the funny question I asked myself
rhetorically, as I laughed out loud heartily.
A smile lingered on my face, as I speculated to myself
about the sequence missing from this dream,
how the Buddha must have entered into my room;
like his entrance into my consciousness, so opportune
in my pilgrimage to unravel God's creative scheme.
But this dream was not so deep to bring me
any peace. Did he come, I wondered quizzically, as he
is frequently portrayed, resembling the little statute

I had placed upon my office desk many years ago;
the Buddha walking mindfully with a small cloth
traveling bag dangling from the crooked stick
his right hand held tight like a stubborn tree
withholding treasured leaves before they fall,
and his migrant's bag filled with meager traveling goods
that often lay across a bare rounded shoulder casually?
"How extraordinary," I uttered to my new visitor, another
soul extraordinaire; this one lately come to provoke
an inquisition in my mind, to prod my spirit quest
and push the barriers of my emergent philosophy.
"You, like the teacher just departed - fleeing,
rushing fast beyond the reaches of my dream -
spurred a movement that spawned a new religion
that founders aimed to use to keep the masses satisfied,
but their apostacies chafed your soul with injury,
a homicide of your original intent. Then fervent followers
recorded their interpretations, proselytized your teaching
into a system of beliefs, they had vested in, complete
with dogma, ritual and practices that monastic monks,
living out their lives in cloistered cells, formed
with a single purpose to withdraw from ordinary lust
and passion, and from want, to embrace a solitary
antiseptic way of life dedicated to muting desires, dread,
and the delimiting ego-centric accoutrements of self-esteem."
"Like your friend, the blessed prophet of love
and peace born of obdurate Israel, I, too, sought
to spread the word that a path was available
for awakened souls to follow individually,
that they might find freedom from the pain
and suffering universal to life on earth, attendant
to all the physics of our evolving universe,"
replied the Buddha sitting comfortably at my bedstead.
"The paths were, however, quite different," I replied
to the humble teacher-monk who was seated near to me.
"First, and most importantly, your followers never

claimed for you the mantle of divinity that Christians
have bestowed upon their Prince of Peace; they say
that he, and only he, can be the path to bring about
the end of pain and suffering, but only in another world
after death. But Buddhists learned a different path
from you: that in awareness and an awakened state
each and all of us individually, must seize the moment,
live in the now, for it is only there man might find
the very essence of living every second in a gifted day."
The Buddha held his posture steadily as I
proceeded to expound upon a set of contrasts
and comparisons I ascribed to each of them.
"Christ, the carpenter, was a common laborer,
while you were a wealthy prince whom your father
sought to isolate from the pain and suffering
that plays out upon creation's grand chaotic stage.
Then, to you came awareness of three realities
and a way of life that offered some escape
from the misery that comes with illness, age,
decay, death, and disintegration into nothingness.
That is when you turned, like Christ, to the appeal
of the ascetic, and a withdrawn, contemplative life.
But like the Christ, you the Buddha freed yourself
from the restraints that tie the hands of reclusive men.
Compassion sped its nutrients coursing through
your blood, its energy overwhelmed your soul
and pushed your mind to open nature's seeing eye,
to emancipate we lonely creatures with senate minds
who give awareness of and birthing life to God.
You both were teachers offering different paths
that women and men might traverse to find freedom
from the human curse—the dread of pain
and suffering, the fear of illness, aging, decay
and death, and the unwelcome demise of joy
and its romantic, soothing balm that eases minds
and lifts the souls of fragile mortal men."

The Buddha smiled warmly, and then replied,
"it's the Middle Path that I discerned
as insight spoke to me while I meditated
underneath a ficus tree, and entered deep inside
an opening into a crease in time. In my trance,
I saw how moderation is the only pathway,
the awakening that turns us from extremes
and does not countenance, nor luxuriate
in selfish, egotistical self-indulgence,
or embrace an austere life, less well-lived;
a life warped by the cruel and gory miscarriage
that flows out of a sad, addictive, unforgiving
absolute denial of the wonderous majesty
of our unique, remarkable, unduplicated self."
"Yes, but there was more to your awakening
than the awareness of the Middle Path,"
I inquired of the master meditator.
"Did you also not blow out the eternal flame
of suffering and of pain, and free yourself
from the folly and the lust embodied
in the circle game of life, death and rebirth?"
"You are right my friend, there is much more
within the insight of the Awakening," the Buddha
said in return, "in that meditative trance-like immobility,
I awakened purged of mankind's common disability;
the desperate time of drawing our last breath,
the overriding, ever-present dreaded fear of death."
For a moment silence filled the surrounding air,
then the Buddha made what seemed a simple dare,
"do you see what both your Christ and I awakened to?"
I could not, no matter the effort I could mount,
find the answer to what now seemed to be a riddle
posed by the Buddha to confound my unsure mind.
The Buddha smiled reassuringly as I just shrugged
my shoulders, surrendering the answer back to him.
"When your Christ, Jesus, said 'it is done,'

he found his elusive liberation and peace.
And when I awakened, I too found tranquility.
I was liberated from the game of circles;
the spiraling constant cycle of death and rebirth.
I cast aside the duality in the comfort and the curse
of belief or doubt in an enduring self. I repulsed
man's fear of change and the compulsion to cling
to things and not concede to change and the specter
of the dark lord of the night and his vanquishing
our hope for some enduring light and precious life."
"But how," I asked the Buddha, "do you reconcile
this insight with your concept of emptiness,
a precept many open-minded souls find barren,
hopeless and vacuous of value, undermining
the fundamental merit within a universe of life?"
"Don't you see," the Buddha asked quickly.
"Reality cannot escape the path of constant change.
Nothing stays the same beyond a single moment;
the flickering of a candle's flame, the life and death
of species, planets, stars and galaxies; each
living in their moment, not enduring eternally.
What I meant by emptiness is unfortunately,
widely misconstrued," the Buddha pointed out,
as I lay enthralled with my unexpected opportunity.
"I heard the Prince of Peace say, earlier to you,
that heaven is the embodiment of moral action
taken in the 'Now.' How is that different
from my Nirvana and the realization that nothing
but the moment exists?" Before I could
think on how best to respond, the Buddha
in merciful compassion said, "the universe
is filled with emptiness; the past is gone
and cannot resurrect itself, and the future
is an illusion whose time may never come.
It's only in the emptiness of the moment
that value can obtain. Heaven and Nirvana

are imputed to human moral conduct,
confined to passages of life traversed
along the Middle Path." The Buddha paused,
then said to me, "I will try another way to bring
you peace, to liberate your mind and free
your strong, brave, endangered, non-enduring soul.
You must find your bliss in the keen awareness;
that man, the thinker who created God; the we,
with all our senses of sight, and sound and touch,
will never fathom the how or why of creation's
confounding mystery. This enigma is unsettling,
it is the great conundrum that even the God
of human ingenuity may never understand or know.
Perhaps, the teacher you adore, best says it right
captured in the wisdom in his tome that spoke
heroically of the fearless Cretan saviors of the gods,
who bore the burden bravely, and did not acquiesce
to hope, or seek in terror to refute the sublime
truth of what is real and what exists."
I closed my eyes to reflect upon what some
must view as the profane possibility the Buddha
had proposed for me to consider and contemplate upon.
I did not meditate for long. I kept my eyes closed,
as insurance not to forget the response, I had
mindfully constructed and composed. Then
as ready as I could be, I said to the Buddha:
"some say that hell is the eternal separation
of an undeserving man from his just god,
but, to me, the bitter often unobserved irony,
is that man and his many fickle gods,
and the grandeur of the universe exist together
only in the consciousness of a single human mind."
I opened my eyes to see the Buddha's face
before he had time to react to my reply,
but he was gone. He had vanished.
Now he was missing from the ever changing,

shifting contours of my dream. "Damn,"
I said in anger, "the cup is emptied
of the past so soon; was it ever truly full,
was the Buddha and his visit actually real?"
I asked these questions without hope of pity
for the living, for a long-suffering mankind,
and for my still uncertain doubtful self.
I was not alone, but it was some time ago,
it seemed to me, since I had a visitor
enter into my room, or were the unexpected
guests just figments of a tantalizing dream?
My wife and children still were near.
They looked weary, as if they hadn't slept
and I wondered if my restless dream kept
them from the sleep that we all need.
But tired or not, they did not leave my side,
as I often heard them call me dad and dear.
Ah, I thought to myself, I saw that white robed
medicine man before. He always seems to
enter into my room with a stethoscope draped
precariously around his neck. I could not be sure
but he did not appear to me to demonstrate
he knew much about the shaman craft.
No sooner had I had that thought,
my judgement was in full retreat.
I heard the white robed one say quietly,
"I'm not sure, no one really knows, but
my instinct is that patients who cannot speak
or move still might hear and understand
reassuring words coming from a familiar voice."
Oh, almost too late, I realized reality was mixed
into my dream, or better yet the dream
I had was an interlude intruding into my reality.
I heard my children say, "we love you, dad,"
and my wife say "I love you so much dear,
I don't know what we will do without you."

I wanted to shout out "and I love you, too!"
I wanted to reach out and squeeze their hands
as their loving hands grasped mine so tenderly.
I know I said a thousand times I loved
each of them, and hugged them in an act
of love frequently. But now I wondered
frantically, "was it enough, surely I could
have done more? How many opportunities
did I pass to be more patient and more kind?
What tricks play out in a doubting mind,
but the problem is the same for all,
there is no time for remorse, for
the only time we have is now.
"He's gone," I heard the medicine man say,
"but no one knows for sure what lies
beyond the thin veil separating life
from death, when one begins and ends."
"I'm a scientist but in truth I cannot
say when he will cease to hear you speak
or feel the warmth of a kiss upon his check.
Stay as long as you want before you
leave with your memories," as he walked
out the door and turned the light to dim.
They stayed awhile more, then stood
and took my hand in theirs one last time,
said "I love you," turned off the light
and walked out into a corridor.
The light of consciousness was fading
fast into night. I had only suspicions of what
was next, but one thing I knew, though
I have regrets and debts that I will never pay,
I did not squander time nor waste love
to wallow in remorse, for I lived my life
in the moment, in the now, and that truth
is the awareness I have awakened to,
and nothing more can matter, if life

is once and done or not. What matters
is how we love and act with charity
and kindness toward our fellow man;
what we do to protect mother earth,
her sacred ground, water and air
from plunderers and polluters reckless
and foul; and how we sound out
and rush to freedom's staunch defense
and trample underfoot vile tyranny
into the dust heap of endless time.

TIME KEEPER

No, time keeper, I do not rush
to see the light. Here, all is well.
Do not push, do not pull, I cling
to my mother's womb, and I will
wage a fight, for here I intend to dwell.
I do not seek the light, fearful
harbinger of dreaded fright.
Within the womb, I am free of pain.
Why, timekeeper, should I emerge
if but suffering is all to gain?
No matter how long you persist,
I will with all my strength resist.
If light brings suffering, pain, decay
and death, then why, time keeper,
should I draw a single breath?
Why not in darkness abide, free
from want and tear? Why, timekeeper,
should I, secure and safe, foolishly
emerge to confront suffering and fear?
Leave me be, time keeper!
Do not struggle to set me free.

I am safe, I have comfort and need
no other sustenance.
I am free of want and pain;
I need no savage warrior in vigilant
watch upon my countenance.
Too soon, its shear force cannot
be contained. Like a mighty river
flows that powerful creative surge.
So, breathe, see, hear,
smell, touch and taste, but be
awakened, and be aware.
The time keeper makes haste.
Do not squander, do not waste.
Relentless he comes, this grim warrior
and final arbiter of universal time.
For me, for you, for the earth
and the heavens, for all things,
the mundane and the sublime.
Impermanence is his clarion call.
I can shout no, but his steps are not
forestalled. The time keeper is implacable.
But stop, I have a mind, with reason,
I can brave the inescapable.
While he comes, I summon my eyes,
my ears, my hands, my tongue, my thoughts,
and I write, speak, sing, dance, touch and taste
the Now. He comes but I have the moment.
My cup is not an empty vessel, and I
have no need, no fear; I will not bow.
Yesterday is gone, eviscerated,
never to return. Tomorrow never is,
never promised, never born.
But, now, in this moment
I confess, I am not forlorn.
In the moment, there is water in my cup.
In the now it touches my lips, it satisfies

what once was my unquenchable thirst.
In excitement, I can acknowledge everything
is suffering, and still, in joy I can burst!
Written words, spoken words, lyric poems
and fables, mythic creatures, conversations,
songs and dance; all engage my mind
in joyful celebration of life's fire leaping flame
and refine my spirit to a higher plane.
It's a hard truth that all is impermanent,
transitory, ephemeral—a fog that fades
in morning's light. But, I, a thinking being,
awakened and aware, discern the noble truth—
now let the Buddha's insight ignite, inflame
and then calm my excited, agitated soul.
I, too, have a path to live this life,
despite the truth that suffering,
sorrow, decay and death command
all time and space. It's a heroic path, absent
hope, and yet, this path is not a fool's race;
defiant, man stands erect, beyond parceled
recompense or reward from heaven's grace.
With compassion, charity and love
for human kind, for all creation's breadth,
I can make this solitary journey full
of worth, defying death.
The shadow of Dante Alighieri's curse
has been my faithful catechism guide.
When moral crisis raised its venomous
head, I did not in silence stand aside.
I grasped beloved Nikos's "Cretan Glance."
I made it mine, a shield and lance.
To war, I set my focus on; understanding
that each of us alone bears solemn duty
and responsibility to save all souls,
and spare this world its genocides
despite humanity's most heinous ghouls.

I confront the great and infinite abyss.
I shout with simple human pride,
my journey has been my joy.
I need no final harbor. I sail freely
into the void. I am free!
My peculiar window into eternity
will close. The sun will set. No more,
for me the moment will have passed.
But, I will have lived a life fulfilled,
with modest few regrets.

THE WATCHMAN'S GAZE

The watchman cried out! "Where?"
"Where Poseidon? You, heartless god
of the sea. You jealous thief. What mischief
has come to my vast and formidable fleet,
my great armada that once sailed
in formation upon the Aegean Sea?"
"I heard you slug."
"What an impudent creature,"
Poseidon growled out loud to himself.
"I am a god! And this annoying voice,
it is nothing more than a fish."
"I have lived forever," Poseidon fumed.
"This peevish creature, only yesterday
learned how to crawl, and now
it dares to breath the air above my sea!"
"It is a low-life, lander; a water-traitor,
an absconding scum who like a treasonous
sea snake has scurried off onto the land."
"You are a fool, watchman, for I have scattered
your precious armada across my endless sea.
They now float, a thousand miles apart.
They are like daytime stars, invisible
to your compromised human sight.
Each day your boats sail farther apart,
never to be seen again, by you or any other."
So, it was, the watchman was alone,
within his tiny boat, with sails extending

out, floating, captively, across
an infinite sea of chaotic uncertainty.
Winds, some gentle, glide past Basseterre.
While others, are full-force Aruban gales,
wild things—no wind vin ordinaire.
The fickle wind—"it's the devil game,"
sailors say. It is tormented with Poseidon's
intemperate, vacillating, dour disposition.
The wind, it truly is a confounding mystery:
at times, predictable, prevailing and reassuring;
and then, suddenly capricious, savage, unnerving.
What presence lurks, hidden within the wind?
What force propels the small, imperiled skiff?
Indiscriminately and unsympathetically,
it drifts over calm seas, silk-like smooth
as polished ivory, into menacing swells
responding to the elephants' anguished cries.
Merciless Poseidon, indignant, is moved
in uncommon compassion by the elephants'
just laments. But mortal man, the giant slayer,
consumed with greed and avarice, musters
no remorse. "It's natures law, the strong prevail,"
says the simian's emergent cousin; an infant
with a nascent brain strained in missing maturity,
still muddled, insensible and too often obscene.
But, amidst this chaos, and defiantly, ignoring
the sea god's angry snipe, the stalwart watchman
casts his pensive eyes across the sea.
His voice remains still, but always on the ready
to shout to his anxious fleet, "land ho!"
With the watchman's eyes in a trance-like stare,
his mind races, dreamlike, to fables
and ancient folklore tales of mythic lands,
where, he reasons with himself, that kinsmen
will in celebration be there to greet him.
The clans stand ready, once reunited, he believed,

to celebrate with him a safe arrival, his return
from that irreverent, cold-bloodied, callous sea.
This heartening gaze for land is the seafarer's
unrelenting, all-consuming, harmonizing dream.
It is there on land, at last, that the sailors
of the sea find the aspirant's muse;
a journey to a place where men and women
revel in passion's lust and love, burst into joyous
song and frenzied dance, and eat and drink unabated
until their appetites are sated. Then, finally there,
exuberant and giddy, drunk from far too many
loaded cups of bold, full-bodied, blood-red wine,
they lose track of toast offered after toast,
to the hosting harbor master's signals to approach.
But other sailing vessels languished far behind.
Obsessed with parchment charts and ocean
passage maps, they abandon curiosity's search –
the mariner's insatiable quest—for adventure,
exploration and discovery's treasures and rewards.
They enslave themselves, and willingly manacle
and shackle their own hands and feet, anchored
to their vessel's unaltered, charted course.
Their lives horribly constricted, are riddled
with insecurities, crippled with dark encumbering
apprehensions. Still, they clung to convention
and would not change their faith-based course
for fear of an uncertain, perhaps, unwelcome end.
These tortured souls are trapped, snared,
prisoners in their fisherman's tangled net.
Their terror is boundless; their great fear
is the unthinkable proposition that a faithful
master will not be found to pay the wages
promised for hard labors, that in good faith,
were performed upon their sea tossed boat.
A cruel fate awaits these poor trusting souls
who will find themselves bound tight in mariner's

rope tied snug to the roughhewn mast,
where mercilessly they will be drawn,
quartered, and then murdered in cold-blood
in unforgiving, self-imposed suicidal despair.
Oh, where are the tears, Poseidon?
Why does Olympus not cry out "foul"
in baleful pain for these tormented ones?
Unfortunate wretches left moored
to an insensible, unacceptable prospect,
which they imposed upon themselves, of
a lonely death, set adrift, upon an uncaring,
hostile sea. These timid sailors, fatigued,
voluntarily expire. They lay down in desperation
and give up their wasted bodies, their fractured
souls to the unrelenting sun's searing heat.
Flesh and spirit scorched, like burnt leather,
their entrails and their souls shrivel.
And Sun, and Wind, and Sea all stand by
indifferently, while forlorn passengers bob
and toss for all eternity upon an infinite,
compassionless, pitiless, unsympathetic sea.
But the brave, the few; they have stories too.
Homer left us with tales of Odysseus, King of Ithaca,
and of his epic journey to Troy and back again
to his beloved Queen, Penelope.
Herodotus wrote of brave Leonidas, King of Sparta,
and his small phalanx of Spartan warriors
who battled Xexres' elite immortals, holding
back a force a million strong until betrayed
at Thermopylae's narrow mountain pass.
Who, among us mortals, could blame
Odysseus' beleaguered men from growing restive.
They were exhausted from raw adventures, and
wary that the perilous voyage back to Ithaca,
so long delayed in route, and difficult to endure,
would take them once again, once too often,

into harsh and unforgiving harm's way.
In such case, they knew their fate, save
for Odysseus; they were sure their flesh
would serve as food for hungry, man-eating fish.
His storm ravaged fleet of twelve Greek ships
had set sail to wage war in Troy. Then, once
homebound, they narrowly escaped a cascade
of harrowing mortal threats. One by one,
the obstacles were overcome: Lotus Eaters,
whose fruit would rob men of their will;
a one-eyed Cyclops; a race of cannibals;
a witch goddess, who would turn gullible men
into swine, tempting them with cheese and wine;
woeful Sirens, whose enchanting melody lured
sailors to a certain death when their ships
struck ragged coral riffs and sank into the sea.
But Odysseus' spirit and resolve could not be
repressed. He, and his depleted fleet, sailed
past danger's reach. The seafaring warriors,
again, defied death's certain claim.
No multi-headed monster, the Hydra,
or Poseidon's inescapable, angry, ocean
whirlpool would keep these spent, intrepid
souls from safely reaching Ithaca's warm embrace
and the voyager king, Odysseus, from holding
Penelope, her bosom to his emaciated chest.
As for brave Leonidas, once Sparta's betrayal
was known, he gathered all the spartan warriors
and said: that for himself there was no choice.
He would stay and fight until his certain death;
and, if others would forfeit their lives,
then Greek cities might have time to unite
and hold back Xexres' massive military force.
"For Sparta and for Spartans, today there
is no middle path," Leonidas warned his men.
"Today, you cannot choose one or the other,

you can only choose freedom and death!"
To the one, the undaunted Spartans shouted
in response: "We give no quarter to our enemy,
and in return, from them, we ask for none."
Leonidas and his Spartan band of hundreds
held the narrow mountain pass until all,
in noble and heroic sacrifice, had died.
But in their wake, tens of thousands of Persians
perished, casualties of spartan swords and lance.
Eventually, the invaders were defeated at Salamis
on the sea, and retreated infamously with
the king-god Xexres back to ancient Babylon.
In honor, and without fear of struggle,
pain or death, these two kings of Greece
tamed their own wild souls. Each man,
acknowledged, heroically aware, that death
holds neither promise or dread, if life is lived
fulfilled. Instinct, intuition and insight
were their faithful guides to the deeply hidden
message that the gods so jealously guard;
the blissful awakening that the gift of life
is its own goodly cause. Stripped of pretentious
arrogance, and emboldened in battle-tested
confidence, these brave noblemen embraced
their different fates. Each stood undeterred,
and stared into the infinite abyss, and shouted
out a trumpeter's warning to all who might
be brave enough to hear and bear the truth:
"I am a man. I am free."
"My journeys, filled with joy, suffering,
conquests and defeats have been my soul's
most true and faithful companion."
And, if you listen closely, you can hear
within the wind that swells above
the white-capped waves, and whistles
hauntingly through a mountain pass,

the voices of Odysseus and Leonidas say:
"While we have breath yet to breathe,
there are wrongs to right, oppressed men
to free, kindness, charity and compassion
to parcel out, and love to freely give.
Now, set your sights ahead men,
for we sail or march, as duty calls,
far beyond the watchman's gaze,
out beyond freedom's bounds."

ABRAHAM'S TRINITY

Five times a day they shout out,
in response to a muezzin's call,
and other times without a cleric's
voice broadcast from a minaret;
followers casual and devout,
in prayer toward the east
they kneel and bow, and then
say Allah Akbar, "God is Great."
The daily practiced ritual unfolds;
the same for those consumed
within the burning fire of belief,
or fearing charges of blasphemy
and apostacy pretend in ceremonial
formality to accept ascribed beliefs
they do not in conscience hold.
To the West the Muslim faith
is demon cursed, a breach
from hell loosed on Christian
innocents. They're infidels,
the mullahs shout, condemning
all who do not pledge Mohamed's
allegiance to the Holy Koran,

its harsh and cruel sharia law.
In crazed revenge these holy men
ascribe a Fattah to make war holy,
a crusade against those outside
the cult of Muslim brotherhood.
But wait before you cast the killing
stones that slay entrapped women
accused alone of adultery; push
the pause button to pernicious hate
for you cannot claim the high ground
and like a snake in weeds slither
across the low ground simultaneously.
Listen to the tortured winds of fate
that call out religious bigotry and hate;
hypocrisy echoes through the treacherous
mountain peaks it must in faith navigate.
Oh, the wind roars its disdain.
Can anyone not hear Verona's
Prince repeat his refrain of woe?
Then hear it now, observe the scourge
that lays upon your hate, that kills
the joy of love, as kinsmen –
Jews, Christians and Muslims,
humans all, are killed in hate,
and heaven cries while God
in righteous anger, dragon fire
in his anguished voice, roar's out
the eternal curse that "all are punish'd."
The West has been too quick
to cast indignant stones upon
Islam's sons and daughters, kinsfolk
all born of the tribe of Abraham.
Their common roots are found
in the oldest western testament,
where God was said to come
like a wind sweeping in to fill

the formless void of a dark
unshapen universe with a burst
of light, a colossal bang and spark
igniting life with particles of energy
thrust out from a point of singularity.
And, God rejoiced when sensate
beings wrote on ancient papyrus scrolls
epic tales of the role they ascribed
to creation's master builder architect,
the grand designer of this beginning.
This they attributed to the great spirit,
the creator of the beginning and the end,
whom they pictured in their dreams,
envisioned in their consciousness,
and put flesh on bones with words
they composed, reflecting faces
in water rippled images of themselves.
And, I say unto all who have ears
opened to the truth to hear:
Oh, Israel, do not call the Prophet's
faith barbaric, cruel and false.
Did not your God command
his servant Abraham to take
his only son, the child Isaac
(his lineage freed, no more
a captive of a barren womb)
to a mountain desolate to slay,
a sacrifice by knife and corpse
to burn, to the sate the thirst
for blood that motivates his God?
Your testament goes on and on,
spewing curse upon curse
that your God weighs upon
those who breach his covenant,
the contract of adhesion he
exacts for loyalty and fidelity.

Who is this God of Israel?
Is he not the willful guardian
at the city gate who casts out
a son who does not heed
his parent's words, a stubborn child
who has grown to manhood
with a mind that reasons on its own,
is by the elders stoned to death
to purge his evil from their midst?
How is it that such cruel will
does not offend the heavens
this God espouses, as a father,
to love, protect, and to defend?
How, you defenders of this faith,
can this transgression withstand
and not admit to shame?
Too many among us share blame;
so, too, for the Christian right;
the swords once held in crusader's
hands have been passed to a new
breed of zealous ones whose
religious bigotry in hatred manifests
a loathing of all that might connect
to their Muslim kin, their cousins
in ancestry linked to Abraham,
while others blame their Jewish kin
in history filled with persecution,
and pogroms ending in fiery kilns.
It is the curse of fundamentalism,
loosed on earth among these three
branches of the tree of faith testified
in ancient texts that began with Genesis,
and now is perverted in a modern exodus
from rationality, compassion and tolerance,
while humanity stumbles backwards
precariously toward terror's dark abyss.

Oh, Christian hypocrites, how is it
you have not drowned in the poisoned
waters of the Pharisees' hypocrisies?
You slay your Savior on his cross,
again, he dies, murdered for your sins,
your crimes against humanity,
the souls that he, in pain and suffering
sought with life and limb and soul
to save, to comfort and consol.
Your bigotry, your misogyny,
your hatred and homophobic hysteria,
your radical racial and religious superiority
offend the Jesus some have said
came into this world, gentle, meek
and mild. But I see a wild man,
his passion pouring like the flooding
stream Sir Walter Raleigh wrote
of to his queen. I see a warrior seeking
redress as treason seems to prosper
while apostates claim false allegiance
to his ascending path to heaven's gate.
Misery comes to you, you missed
his point, your inquisitions still persist
without the ghastly fire and the stake
but just as deadly to the body
and the soul of sacred human lives.
You have grown deaf and blind
to the words of the son, whose
father sacrificed him to ease
his own offended mind;
for gentle Jesus did not bear
the cross of crucifixion to purge
your petty sins or free his father's
twisted, troubled, melancholy mind.
Your Savior, Christ the warrior,
was a prince of peace, and blessed

the poor, the meek, the hungry,
the sick in need of comfort,
the pure in heart, the merciful,
those who make the peace.
Today, the ministers who lead
their Christian congregations in praise
and song, sing Gloria in excelsis Deo,
and Glory to God in the Highest, while
worshiping the son within their holy trinity.
But the martyred son reserved
his highest praise for blessed souls
who looked to common bounds
and did not bow to hate and bigotry
to those outside their clan or cult.
For what reward, he asked,
should a man expect to love only
those who love them, or to greet
as neighbors' brothers and sisters,
but not say to weary strangers
traveling from some other place,
hello, my new friend, you and all
who flee from tyranny and war
are kin to us and welcome here to stay.
For is it not so, As-Salam-Alaikum,
and Shalom Aleichem, spoken in Arabic
and Hebrew means "peace be unto you"?
And did not Christ, Jesus say,
"peace I leave with you?"

OPEN TABLE

The youthful master, in joy's glowing halo,
approached his father's loyal servants,
"last evening, my brother, my father's

oldest son returned from a banishment
self-imposed, and father in his exuberance
restored the covenant he had pledged;
while my mother, with tears streaming
down her checks, wrapped her arms lovingly
around my brother, drew him to her bosom,
and held her hug in an ecstasy impossible
to contain," said the young master happily.
"My father wishes to hold a celebration
and host a festive open table, as he, too,
can hardly contain his joy in surrendering
suffering's long malaise. Father is delighted,
and relieved, for our good fortune that my
brother; the lost and wandering prodigal,
has at last come home," said the youthful
master, whom the servants idolized.
Then he instructed his father's servants,
"rush to the village, announce my brother's
return and the feast that is to follow."
The servants, wanting to avoid an error,
asked the man they called *rabbi,* beloved
teacher, "who master, whom within the village
should we to invite to your father's table?"
"Why, all the people of course," replied
the young master. "Father has instructed us
to set enough tables for all the village people
to join the celebration rejoicing in my absent
brother's unexpected return. Our tables
will be loaded with food fresh from market
and the best of father's early harvest wine."
A few servants, newer to his father's service,
sheepishly inquired. "Young master, it is,
is it not, the prosperous, upright and loyal
of the village, that we should summon
to be your father's honored quests?
Surely, he does not want the celebration

tainted by the baser elements that haunt
the village hovels in the ghetto and the slums?"
An older servant, stooped from life's long labors,
but well respected by his peers, interjected
"you have not served this master long enough
to know, the rabbi, and his father and his mother
draw no distinction between rich and poor,
enemy or friend. Now hurry, spread the word
to every villager that they are invited
and welcome at this sumptuous event."
The young master smiled, and gently said,
"old Malik is right. On this day, father wishes
that no one be slighted. On this day, no one
has class status or special benefit.
We are today, as is witnessed across
the nighttime sky, one people, all the same,"
said the young rabbi, so wise beyond his days.
"Everyone will be welcomed by my father
and our family. All he asks, imploringly,"
continued the teacher, "is that enemies
put aside their grievances and their hatred,
and bring along a heart filled with charity
and compassion, and share our boundless joy
that my lost brother and their beloved
son, Lucifer, has returned to us."

A DEPTH TOO DEEP TO SEE

The curling tops of white capped waves
gleam in the glow of a lunar night;
a sea-frothed undulation of phantom light
that locks my eyes and tugs my mind.
The rolling sea provokes a soulful sense
of motion to a vast, deep unfathomable
well of azure seas and blue-blooded oceans.
In calm or stormy seas, I hear, and see,
and smell and taste its salty essence.
But my senses disappoint; the guarded,
jealous ocean hides its deepest secrets.
Neither my senses, nor I their captive
commander can penetrate its greatest depth.
There the wary watcher in the water stays,
in mystery and in awe, inscrutable and safe.
Like dangling sentences standing alone
at a loss to form a single paragraph,
I am left to gaze with no tools of deeper
exploration save for nascent human intuition.
It is my human, all too human flaw; so deep
the sea, I cannot see or know its greatest depth.

OUT OF DARKNESS

Out of darkness bursts man.
Each living, breathing, sensing,
searching soul is pushed and shoved,
then pulled from its safe keeping
within its nurturing mother's womb.
Thrust into light's first blinding glare
our primal root, our safety cord,
is severed. And so, begins our life's
precarious journey, as sailors on the sea
and pilgrims trudging upon the land.
We are here, scarcely for a fleeting moment;
our infinitesimal interlude of scarce time.
We lapse so quickly, hardly accustomed
to the light that warms our mother earth.
Then, once again, without our acquiescence,
roots once planted optimistically, in trusted
ground are seized, and wrenched and torn
from our adopted mother, planet earth.
Then back to darkness we return;
not discarded to the dark abyss
from whence we came; not entombed,
but reclaimed, nestled tight within
our mother earth's accepting womb.

OF DAY, AND NIGHT, AND GOD

I look to the heavens, with awe
and open eyes. I push my mind
to its limits, but still, I can't decide.
I struggle to apprehend thy divine,
holy presence. Like a homicide detective,
I search intensely for corroboration.
I want to find you, *God of Gods*,
to clearly see your face in focus.
I want to know your essence,
confirm it's not a cruel façade.
But I must question, as a thinking man,
will I ever comprehend, with reassuring
certain knowledge, the nature of the mystery?
My brain, with reason and intuition,
is my tool for exploration and discovery.
It seems so insufficient for the task
of revealing your timeless sacred essence;
your presence, invisible and hidden outside
the distant outposts of my tormented mind.
And yet great creator, I do not despair.
Nor do I grow anxious as evening nears.
For truly, I believe, that night should hold
no fear or dread, or some unwelcome,
unexpected recompense or surprise.
Night, I have determined, is not a thing
of sinister despair. Night, like dawn awakened,
is but another mask of the universal journey

to light, and then, back again, to night.
This should be no cause for sadness
or pathological remorse. Profound, yet
amazingly simple, this is our living nature.
We are stardust creatures, and we share
a similar fate; not unlike, though infinitesimally
shorter than a beam of light from a dying star,
that bursts and spreads across the Milky Way.
This unsettling fact strikes fear in the minds
and hearts of many. But if a man has been
awakened, in a state of blissful awareness,
then he will not cry out that providence
is unjust. Now conscious in a heightened state,
the awakened man recognizes impermanence
reigns supreme. He applauds the wisdom
of the great creative force; the surge to birth.
His ethereal existence provides the heroic
opportunity to defy his fate, and within
his intervening moment leave behind
a world that is a better place. And then,
in pride stripped bare of every trace
of arrogance, such a man or woman
can say bravely to their god:
I can choose to live with pride and joy.
I can be a force for love, compassion, and charity.
I can do this, if I choose, for all humanity.
I can do this for all creation's wonders.
I can do this if it is my determined will.
I have wrestled with God and the devil
and that great battle has set me free.
Now I can return to your bosom, my mother
earth; beyond any place where pain
and suffering can intrude, and life's love
and labor's rest is reward enough.

THE WOLF'S LAMENT

I hear the haunting, forlorn cry
of a lone wolf's sad lament
break the silence of the night.
The creature's tortured howl
intrudes upon our startled ears.
All whom hear the eerie interruption
of the silence in the night, fear
the mournful dirge is meant for them.
The proud grey wolf's mate for life,
now lies dead from a hunter's bow.
Its baleful cry mourns for moments
missed that now are lost to fate's
cruel twist. The time they once shared
is cast away like vaporous winds of war.
Nature wanes to impotence. Its creative
mastery of time and space cannot
reconnect the grey wolf with its mate.
As minutes pass between its painful
wails, each silent pause serves to frame
a melancholy lament of the squandered
moments that pass imperceptibly beyond
its desperate grasp. If words were scribed
on paper, that spoke to the noble wolf's
despairing howl, they would speak
painfully of the tragic theft and cruel,
fierce murder of metered time.
The wolf's howl cries out, a haunting

taps played at a soldier's grave,
sounds memorializing a time once
shared but now will never come to be.
The joyless wolf, whose highbred life
has been purloined and sabotaged,
is now condemned to lonely solitude.
Its plaintive wowl sounds out
a warning light that alerts man
and beast astute enough to discover
the meaning distilled within its call.
The gritty grey's canine descendants
understand its loss implicitly,
far better, I believe, then you and me
with all our attributed intellectual capacity.
A dog's life is a living testament
to reality's harsh and stingy truth,
that there is nothing noble or heroic
in ceding ground to lonesome solitude.
The wolf's domesticated cousins,
ten thousand years removed in time,
surpass their human masters' childlike
perceptions that fall short of the sublime.
Our canine friends, adaptive descendants
of the highborn wailing wolf, intuitively
perceive that comfort and happiness
are hammered into being on an anvil
of sacred sharing of aberrant time and space,
and of loving commitments made despite,
and in utter defiance of our solitary fates.

WHO HEARS THE SILENCE OF MY SOUNDS?

Sun rises and then it sets,
the burning orb comes and goes
easily, without suspicion
or harboring a modicum of regret,
while I acknowledge painfully
I cannot deny or hold off
the giant ball of turbulence
from its appointed path as it glides
effortlessly across our Milky Way.
It's true that night relents,
gives way to day, silently
without a herald's shout,
while I struggle hard to suppress
and keep the uncompliant onslaught
of demanding messages away.
There is a war that rages
unrelentingly within myself
and I alone, a solitary sentential,
the gargoyle at the gate,
must keep me safe
and off the center stage,
where I will otherwise
repeat lines from manic scripts
that to an unaccustomed ear,
unsettlingly, sound strange.
I hear the obstinate commands
that tell me I must count and count

and then recount again, before
I step across a sidewalk crack.
The voice within and I, its enemy,
fight throughout the day
until exhausted from the fray
explode in anger at this curse
or implode and then collapse
and find an elusive peace
within sleep's comforting reprieve.
As detrimental as this might sound,
I still have means to resist,
to block my ears and turn away
like Odysseus trying mightily to resist
Circe's island sirens' deadly call.
But the ticks that twitch and shake
and the noise that emanates
that startles and annoys,
cruelly come involuntarily.
On solemn oath and testament,
I swear, if I only could,
I clearly would,
you should surely recognize,
hold them back so not
to draw attention to myself.
I ask that kindness and compassion
come to me, and give to you the same,
for no one knows the sounds
that cry out for expression in the silence
of the messages encoded in my brain.

THE LAST JUDGMENT

Oh, you tortured soul, stare down,
peer far into the deep water's sleep:
your eyes squeezed shut, tight,
within their sculpted hallow holes,
resist the tug and nagging pull,
hold fast, try hard to not overthink.
Your ears are poised on a hunted
animal's high alert and hear the ocean's
carnal sighs, the sorceress sirens' call
seductive in your melancholy gloom.
But I shout out, "you must beware
of desperation's false equivalency,
stop, do not apply the numbing salve,
do not purchase hastily, at a price
too high to pay, delusion's sabotaging
thought to leap. Oh, troubled soul
do not leap from your vessel's
lowest deck, to die, defying nature's
ascribed genetic code to struggle
and survive; to plunge down, to sink,
to sleep you think, back before life's
emergent ooze, finding safety once again
within the confines of your mother's
nourishing, warm protective womb.
The waves hypnotic dance, like Niagara's
rapids' rushing to its thunderous fall,
entice your martyred mind with fanciful

illusions of pain's retreat and suffering's
end. But a harsher truth is locked
and loaded within a mind that's crucified.
It marches step by step, arm in arm
in the unending suffering of the chronically
unsatisfied. Despite the faithful's stubborn
search, it is a fruitless enterprise;
and revelation delivers the complicating
news - there is no golden fleece,
no holy grail, no odyssey will take us
to fields of flowing grain in fabled Elysium.
Defiantly, at the edge of nothingness,
impermanence withstands, a bulwark
at the precipice; regeneration's impersonal,
chaotic gift: universe to universe
for galaxies in wild spiral spins;
and stars aflame that only later
explode and then retract and implode;
and planets fair and hostile, too;
snow-capped mountains touching clouds;
and salty oceans vast with a storied past;
and fresh water lakes and raging
rivers rapids running wild, and plants
and animals sustaining life until its final
gasp, only to be incinerated when the sun
expands. And sensate humans, too –
all tied, one to one, with strings
that stretch across the universe,
drawn to warm light's luminosity,
afraid of night's approaching dark,
sometimes violent, always silent
last imploding act. I beg my friends,
unknown and known, resist the plunge,
hold back the pain and castigating urge,
embrace creation's truth, if truth
there is, that none, no-self, endures

beyond the fleeting moment's grasp.
Give up, ascend, abandon venturous hope
and cast aside self-deception's reverie
that suffering ever ends, and hold within
the only hands you have to touch and feel
and gather earth's early harvest grapes,
and drink the blood-red consecrated wine
of life from the ripened juice within
that imperiled sacred cup. Gulp, taste
and savor, feel the power and the gentle
grace of life's alluring sweet antidote;
its one eternal moment in the mind
for those who are awakened in the night,
who see and hear and are aware, and push
from conscious recognition the bloody hands
of unforgiving guilt, and move beyond
to a clearer state of mind, and enlightened
conquer fear's most dreadful fright.
Bodies turned to trees eternally
is not the fate that God himself
unmercifully decreed for suicide.
Dante's slant on punishment divine
is skewed and out of meter and of rhyme.
It's loss of singularity's originality,
where one and only one life luminous
can lift a spirit to a higher plane,
transform the matter of its unruly mind
and ailing soul—trapped within its mortal
space—and carry forward God's primordial,
evolutionary code as ancient homo sapiens
once raised new born children high above
their heads and holding them in outstretched
arms called out to their impassive gods:
"this one, this daughter, this son,
is born today to live and carry on
that I might live and breathe beyond

my numbered days, in this child's wondrous body, mind and soul."
This is enough for me, for this theorem that I postulate, my dear but troubled friends is our Paradiso.

THE OLD HOME CEMETERY

A white post fence nestles close,
adjacent to the edge of a natural
deciduous forest, centuries old.
Within its fold, row upon row
of weathered headstones unfold.
I slowly open the cemetery gate
and enter tentatively within.
My eyes are drawn momentarily
to a thick, surrounding forest canopy
and gaze upon the stately sentinels
that stand and shade the holy ground.
These proud sentinels - green capped
in summer time, gave off life sustaining air,
which along with nature's gift of rain
sustained their once living charges.
The stoic trees bore silent watch
and witness for decades passing by;
until, some after a century of labor's
unflagging duty were unceremoniously
discharged, recalled and fell, crashing
silently to the forest's verdant floor,
where they now lay while others grow
to take their post along the forest's edge.
Step after step I pass by a stone marking
out a place of rest beneath my feet.
The marker calls out to me that someone
who once walked above the ground,

now lies in rest within the earth's embrace;
held tight as a mother snugs a child
close to her soft consoling breasts.
They are there now; the markers
tell me so. I pause while my mind
considers in its own unhurried time
how best to frame and then to ask
the questions that no grave marker
alone can ever satisfactorily answer.
Are you there? If not, where?
And where pray tell were you and I
before we walked upon this earth?
And what of the planets, the night stars
and galaxies eons come and gone?
Where? Do they not reside somewhere
beyond the awareness of my mind?
The answer is not easily obtained,
but it's impermanence that seems
to reign supreme in our realities.
I sit on a white wooden bench,
and like earth renewed by a steady
summer rain, I absorb the sight,
the sounds, the scents in the air
of the old family Home Cemetery.
It is a place of rest for generation
after generation of my father's
hardy pioneer family. Row upon row
of markers call out their names
and shout out, to all who chance
to happen by: "I, too, once lived,
and breathed, like you, and walked
above this ground that is now my home."
As I gaze out, I know deep within
my soul that stars were born to die;
the case for everyone, including me.
Day does give way to night, eternally.

But, is it not equally so that night too
gives way to day, sunset to sunrise?
Light dawns, life emerges, and the cycle
churns and turns without escape—in rhythm
with life's coquettish universal flux.

OLD WOMAN IN A CHAIR

The old woman wore a faded
silk and cotton blended blouse,
dimmed from weekly washing;
a shabby shell, its color vanquished
from daily battles with sun's bright light.
She watched the flashing screen
pronounce its hawking pitch.
Her stoic face a bulwark of resistance
to pent up emotions conditioned release.
And neither pain or joy was betrayed
or loosed that the old man
could easily discover or trace.
She sat within the sturdy chair,
its warranty long ago had lapsed.
She clung to it like a royal throne
passed on to kings and queens,
but never gave a hint or clue
to her silent, dark despair.
She shook her head, a heavy
sigh inserting disdain into the air.
She heard the huckster's tainted claim,
"its cream would, like a miracle,
the spots of age, repair;
just watch the scarlet letters
age had tolled simply disappear."
But in the silence of her suffering
and her pain, the old women

knew the story's ending better;
she felt as kin to the Lady queen
who shouted out, "out, out
damned spot," as she rubbed
her hands fanatically back and forth;
the envy of the water wizard searching
frantically for life's liquid gold,
buried underground, a water well
that hides out just above
the gates that lead to the first
descending rings of hell.
The shaman claims assurances,
this is the place where she can find
the source that births and saves
all plants and animals from burning
at the stake and death's decay.
The old man grasps her hand
in his and asks, "what's wrong,"
and she just shrugs, tries to smile,
and replies, "I just don't feel well."
"How so," he implores in anguished
pain to his lifelong mate and friend;
while she delays thinking to herself,
'Oh love, my clock is winding down,
I feel it in my bones and limbs;
it's the toll of age that grinds our bodies
and our minds into a sandy residue.
It's the fate that all confront,
the reaper's grim avoided call.'
She says to him, "it's nothing dear,
it's only age related, common things."
But deep within her burdened mind
her soul cries out silently to the God
whose chaos tangles human fate,
"my pain and suffering are born
within the humble joy this old man

has brought to me and that soon
will necessarily come to a most
unwelcome closing end."
She takes his long familiar hand
in hers, her fingers entwined in his,
and says, "I love you, dear,
I'm fine today, just old,"
then she turns and looks away
toward the flat rectangular screen.
He turns toward a table tray
for water for his lady queen,
and unaware misses' cues
to her suffering silent scream.

Fiction

Fiction

The Desert Beast

THE BEAST OF THE desert ate insects, most often locust, hard-crusted stale bread, and honey. The honey was a treat for him. It came, strangely enough, when a frightened villager gave a small portion to him as alms in the hope the beast would accept the gift and quickly move on to terrify others. Alone, on the outskirts of Jerusalem, he would sit, wait for the sun to begin its nightly retreat toward the western horizon. He would reach into a weathered leather pouch that was slung over a shoulder with a hemp strap and hung like an appendage close to his body. Always, out of etiquette and concerns for cleanliness, seldom observed or thought likely of the beast by others, his right hand would slide into the pouch for the extraction work. He had large hands, but the pouch was deep enough that his right hand entered without much resistance. Once in, his fingers, strong and sinewy like the hemp strap, would scoop out, with surprising dexterity, a handful of insects. Then the nightly ritual would begin. First, he would look at the bug that was grasped viselike, between two fingers that resembled a scorpion's pincher claws. Then with a slow arch of his hand he would toss the insect, dead or alive, silent or shrieking, into the dark confines of his brown-stained, toothy mouth. Next up, when he had the delicacy, was a dab of Honey. Because he was alone, only he could hear the crunch, as he chewed and slowly turned the insects into a mushy paste; just like churning butter. The honey, when he had it, sweetened the taste. Honey or not, the villagers would whisper outside of the beast's hearing, that a goat would vomit if it was forced to eat the beast's choice of a meal. The beast did his part to rid the land of the giant grasshoppers that spread out in swarms and devoured all but the most intractable vegetation in their path. But the impact on the total population of the plant destroying insects was negligible, nothing impeded their efforts to strip the landscape to the bare soil.

Everyone feared this hairy desert beast. Children, who overheard their parents hushed conversations about the monster that devours men, were terrified of the untamed wild man from the desert. They would run shrieking in terror if they had a chance encounter during one of the desert beast's infrequent trips into Jerusalem to visit the Temple. He was taller, by nearly the length of a sandal, than his Hebrew brethren and the Roman occupiers. He had dark eyes, black as a deep cave, that protruded outward from their sockets. Everyone tried to avoid eye contact with the beast. Most people shuddered at the prospect of having to look directly at his face. They would say to themselves, "he can see right through you, he can peer into a person's soul." The great fear was that the ogre would see past a person's conscious mind; the vigilant sentinel and one of man's elaborate defense mechanisms that obscure the real person buried deep within our outward appearances and guarded words. Let that fiend stare into your eyes for the briefest moment, people would fret, and he will see your soul and all its petty secrets and moral regrets. "It's a bad omen," people would mutter to their neighbors, "if the seeing eye of the beast latches on to you." If such was your misfortune, people swore that bad luck would surely follow. Some in private terror, too frightened, to even whisper to a wife or husband, were convinced the ghoulish beast was the devil's agent come to harvest souls for a mournful journey to Hades.

People find convention, ordinary appearances, and predictable behavior comforting. The unorthodox and chaotic make people uneasy. Extreme eccentricity in appearance, demeanor, and language terrifies men, women and children. The desert beast evoked the same kind of fear that pain and suffering, and aging and death provoke in humans. It did not matter if you were a friend, if he had any is debatable, or an enemy, which he had many; everyone seemed unsettled by the beast's peculiarities. His ghoulish diet was peculiar; his face and body were odd, and his manner of dress defied normal customs and convention.

A lamb skin was girded around his loins, snugged at the waist with a leather strap. He wore sandals that had been worn thin from the abrasive desert sand and rocks during his recurring trips into the desert and his eventual return to Jerusalem. The worn-out sandals did little to hide his hideously calloused feet. The villagers and city dwellers alike speculated that the beast's feet were afflicted with some leprous disease. His austere wardrobe was completed with three trusted accessories; his leather pouch with a hemp strap slung over a shoulder, a slightly crooked wooden staff,

The Desert Beast

and a reed mat and thread bare woven blanket rolled together and tied at the middle and slung over his other shoulder by another hemp strap. He found the reed mat and blanket during an extended journey through the desert. These treasures were near the body of some unfortunate pilgrim who went into the desert to commune with God but instead met up with death. The beast reasoned with himself that the unlucky pilgrim had no further use for such useful items. Surely, the beast told himself, if the dead pilgrim realized his circumstances, he would gladly, out charity and compassion, tell the desert beast to help himself.

If the wild man's tall, lanky frame and haunting face weren't unsettling enough, there was more about his appearance to be observed. His chest was a thick tangled bush of hair, barred to the elements; the sun and its scorching heat, the wind and the abrasive sand that buffeted his uncovered torso, and the rare rain storm which would drench his body with water because he was unable to quickly find shelter. The hair on his head and the beard on his face were unkempt, and an equally tangled mess. These he would rarely trim. When he did, he used a small blade that seemed always to slide to the very bottom of his pouch. His arms and legs were thin, but not spindly and weak. His limbs were strong and sinewy from his daily walks, and the steep climb up the craggy, desert mountains. This he did often, as he left Jerusalem behind, and went searching for a fissure in a mountain where he could rest, and later have his own conversations with Jehovah.

His pilgrimages into the Sinai desert were well known. His enemies within the Temple hierarchy and among the Roman authorities, all hoped he would enter the desert and never return. This would eliminate a major problem from their concerns. The wild man made them uncomfortable. He affected people and that was disturbing to the status quo. The man went into the desert to talk with the almighty, and he believed that Jehovah conversed with him. The man was mad, of this there was general agreement among the ruling classes of the Hebrews and the Roman occupiers. The desert beast, they reasoned, deserved watching. The authorities, religious and secular, worried about the mad and zealots, and they were beginning to question which category best applied to the beast of the desert.

The Jordon River lies approximately twenty miles east of Jerusalem. When the hairy, wild man would ride a desert wind back toward Jerusalem, he would often stop and stay near the river's banks. Standing just offshore, waist deep in the silt laden, murky water, the beast whose given name was John, was known to a few followers and curiosity seekers, not as the desert beast, but as the Baptist. He would stand, his back to the water, his face looking to the shoreline. He could feel on his back the afternoon heat of the giant, red orb that blazed unmercifully on the Galilean landscape. The bearded crocodile was in his element; opening his mouth, barring his teeth to the light, guttural sounds escaping from his belly with terrifying ferocity. The desert beast had morphed into a water monster. And then the thing in the water would find its voice and shout out, always the same alarming admonition to the small gathered crowds. He would shriek, "Be forewarned, the road to Jehovah is a narrow and steep path."

And then, like the prophets of old, his sermon would seemingly pour out of his mouth. "God stands atop the highest mountain peak," he would begin. "To reach Jehovah you must commit to an unending climb. Your journey with be difficult; you will need to ascend steep, unforgiving cliffs that dwarf the mountains of Moab."

His voice rising, its pitch shriller, the beast would howl, "your life, and your salvation depend upon your resolve and your actions; your intent is meaningless to God. Jehovah is a God of action; not words, not rituals, right choices and good acts are what he demands."

Always about this time, the Baptist would ease back. Whether this was out of fear of losing the crowd and sending it scurrying away in fear and depression, or out of seldom expressed but genuinely held compassion for humanity, is open to speculation. There in the water he would continue in a less intimidating tone, "there is, however, good news. You can do this. I know you can. All that God requires is that you take the first step. Reach out your hand and God will cross the breadth of Israel to meet you."

"Can you hear his voice roll in on the desert wind or gurgle up with the flowing river water," asked the Baptist. "His voice is there, and it cries out to you. Listen carefully to the wind and the water; they carry Jehovah's voice. They are his messengers, his tribunes. They call, come take the first step and begin your climb to reach my holy summit." The Baptist paused, and surveyed the crowd, just after saying, "there is no other path."

As he carefully scanned the small crowd he noticed several faces that he recognized. A few he knew by name, and others he knew by position or just through observation. Among those he knew by name were three women, the sisters Miriam and Martha and their friend Sabella; several men who seemed to come and leave with the women, including Aaron and Harel, local fisherman who had returned from their early morning castings; and Mathew, a thin juvenile, always under the watchful eyes of an older brother who stood back from the rest of the gathering. The Baptist did not know the older brother's name but from his looks he thought he might be a laborer, perhaps a mason. He saw Jeremiah, the baker, who was the beast's source of stale, unsold, day's end bread. Ezra, a frowned upon Hebrew, who collected taxes as an agent of the Roman occupiers, was among those on the river bank today. The Temple guardians, unknown to their tax paying brethren, secretly benefited from Ezra's government sanctioned duties, receiving a percentage of the money that went to the Roman Governor General. Standing further back and opposite of Mathew's attentive brother, were two beneficiaries, Roman soldiers (Calvus and Gordianus) who had been assigned for more than a year to follow the comings and goings of the desert beast and report back their observations to their Centurion, Gaius. Finally, there were always the temple agents, the spies of the Temple high priests, Annas and Caiaphas.

The Baptist was aware that if the pause in his preaching was longer, the crowd would disperse. The gathering, fearing that the beast had been searching for the eyes of its next victim were getting restless, most diverted their eyes toward the ground; all, that is, except the Roman soldiers and the Mathew's older brother. These three men were not intimidated by the desert beast. Almost on que, the Baptist resumed his sermon, "the words of God's prophets are a warning."

"Strain your ears to hear their words. Force yourselves to listen to the wisdom of the ancient ones. These sentinels have been sounding the ram's horn of alarm for centuries," entreated the Baptist. "I admit, their voices fell silent long ago, and sand now fills their empty skulls, and blocks their once dry, parched throats. But their wisdom survives. Their words are still carried on the desert wind and flow with the river current. God will not allow their warnings to perish."

"If you will listen, you can hear God's cry; it endures in nature's wake, and calls out to you, 'do not stand by in silence in the face of injustice,'" admonished the Baptist.

"What action does this Wildman call upon the Jewish rabble to take," asked Calvus. "I can't be sure," responded Gordianus, "but Gaius will want to know exactly what this ghoul says to the crowd."

"We should watch the Levites and their spies; their behavior is of interest to Gaius as well," cautioned Calvus.

"You are right Gordianus; the Centurion has ordered us to observe this ugly, unkempt beast and report back everything that transpires. Gaius will not take kindly to our service if we leave out an important detail," said Calvus.

"Gaius sees signs to future events, that lay hidden from other's senses," replied Gordianus. "Gaius is on a fast path to promotion, which is good for us; provided we are attentive to even the most obscure phrase or look," said Calvus.

The Baptist's protruding eyes panned the horizon, passing the roman soldiers, the Levites and their spies, and were about to settle on Mathew's older brother when they were distracted. A voice had called out from the crowd. It was Jeremiah, the baker, a notorious kneader of bread and flesh. He was a stout man with a pointed nose and small eyes that danced with light, passion and mischief. His fine linen robes doing their best to hide his enormous girth. He was a man of enormous appetites. He loved his bread and the money he earned from its sales, but his insatiable lust for flesh outdid his love for bread, and he easily parted with his profits to enjoy daily bartered exchanges with local prostitutes. God, the villagers would joke, had made a mistake; Jeremiah should have been a bull spending its seed, not some blown up baker accumulating weight and wealth.

"But Baptist, aren't you forgetting we are Hebrews, we are Jehovah's chosen people; we have our covenant," Jeremiah retorted.

No sooner had the premature words been uttered, then the baker cursed his own stupidly. *Fool he thought to himself. Why can't I hold my waging tongue? Now I have awakened the monster and his fiery breath will scorch me.* He could feel the heat from the Baptist's burning eyes. *He sees me,* he muttered to himself. *Please, God, save me from the fiend.*

Calvus said to Gordianus, "the stupid baker must be imploring his god to protect him from the coming scourge."

"Did you see how the mad man's eyes turned red? Were they on fire?" Calvus asked excitedly. Gordianus responded, "Gaius will relieve us of our post if we say we witnessed this aberration." Gordianus shaking his head back and forth several times emphatically replied, "I saw nothing," as the Baptist's angry face bore down on the impudent baker.

Jeremiah shifted nervously from foot to foot, his sandals alternately resting on the other's bared toes. Beads of sweat formed on Jeremiah's forehead. His deceptively strong hands—strengthened from the daily rigors of kneading bread—wiped away the perspiration that had rolled down his forehead's slope and gathered, damned at the edge of his overhanging eyebrows.

"I tell you, baker, Jehovah can take the stones that line your ovens and make descendants for Abraham," roared the water monster. The Baptist's body seemed to convulse making a twisted advance toward the shore.

"Claiming lineage to Abraham's seed will not protect you from Jehovah's wrath," shouted the Baptist. "You think Jehovah cares if you are a Hebrew?"

"That means nothing to God," said the Baptist. "Jehovah's covenant is a call to action, to do good, to reject evil. Free yourself from the yoke of sin. Our God requires action. He is not content with words or good intentions. Only your actions matter, people of Israel; our God is adamant, your lives must be defined in truth, justice, charity, compassion, and with a righteous heart."

Gordianus nudged Calvus with his shield, "this we can report to Gaius; again, he calls upon the Hebrews to act."

"Yes, I suppose so," shrugged a slightly annoyed Calvus, silently questioning, what action was the Baptist suggesting the Hebrews should take. Before he asked Gordianus if the Baptist was secretly alluding to insurrection, he quickly suppressed the troubling thought. *There will be a better time to ask this question; I don't trust Gordianus, he will try to report whatever ingratiates him to Gaius to advance his own career. Damned patrician, he inherited his position. He didn't earn it in battle like me.*

Deep down in his belly, a guttural sound of fury was about to be unleashed. The Baptist spit into the air, clearing all the bile that had gathered in his throat. "The axe is ready; the Lord, the Almighty Jehovah, watches. He will, I warn you, cut down all the rotted trees at their roots; even Abraham's roots. The time is coming. God will destroy everything that does not bear good fruit. A fire awaits them, and you too, descendants of Abraham. Only those who follow the path of moral conduct will escape."

The Baptist's memory was like a snare. The ancient sacred scriptures, once heard, were encoded in his brain. He could resurrect the words of a prophet effortlessly, whenever it suited his purposes. Today was such a time. His words flowed with less effort than the current of the river where he now stood; his knees were now exposed in the shallow water closer to the shore. And he stood closer to the crowd.

There were people there, who later would say the Baptist resurrected Isaiah's ghost. By some accounts, thunder clasped, and lighting bolts shot out of the beast's clenched fists as he thrust his arms overhead toward the sky. But that was hyperbole. It was the prophet Isaiah's watchman's claim, that the Baptist summoned on that auspicious day. There would be no stopping him. He was about to give voice to his own version of old Isaiah's prophecy, proclaiming: "For the Lord has said to me: 'You are my watchman. Announce to my people what you see. And, I tell you, wayward people of Israel. I see a nation of citizens who no longer think for themselves. I see sons and daughters who disrespect their parents."

With his right arm extended, and a sinewy finger pointed at the crowd, the Baptist bellowed above the din noise of those gathered at the river's shore. "For an ox knows its owner, and an ass its master's crib; but Israel has forgotten its covenant with Jehovah."

"Though you pray," the Baptist chastised the crowd, "your words are hollow and lack the validation of action. Your hands are stained with the blood of sins and lost opportunities to act as righteous servants of the Lord. You are unclean, and your inaction renders you unfit to stand in God's light."

"For generations, the prophets have told you what is required to reclaim Moses' promised land," explained the Baptist. "A messiah, born of David's blood, waits and watches for Israel to remove evil from its heart; to practice charitable deeds; seek justice; provide alms for the poor and welcome strangers; and defend the fatherless and ease the burden of widows. These are your appointed tasks; do them well and do them often."

Then the river monster turned and shouted at the crowd, while everyone gathered (other than Calvus and Gordianus) thought the beast was staring at them only. "The Almighty, the everlasting Father of Eternity, calls upon you. Those of you who hear his cry, obey his commands, and act as he demands; you will prosper and reap the promises of Israel's covenant with Jehovah. Those who stand idle and do nothing when decency and simple human compassion cry out for your help; you shall be torn into pieces by the Almighty's avenging blade."

"Your life, you simple fools," prodded the Baptist, "must bear witness to your faith in Jehovah. God demands that you behave and conduct yourselves with charity and humility. He made you from dirt and clay and Adam's rib. You were to be a mirror image of his divine self."

The beast knew he had to repeatedly remind the fickle masses to cut through the veil of sin that suppressed human compassion and dignity and throttled individual freedom. The Baptist insisted, the greatest sin was silent acquiescence to injustice and poverty. "Whoever has two shirts must give one to his brother who has none. Whoever has food must share it with his neighbor who has little, and with the stranger passing through who has none."

"And what of me, Baptist? What advice, what solace, can you offer me," asked Ezra. Ezra was a Hebrew, and an agent of the Roman authorities. His official duty was to collect and record the payment of taxes from the people of occupied Israel. The Hebrews hated the heavy tax burden. They called the practice of Roman tribute, robbery. It was an affront to their lost sovereignty, and to Jehovah. But the Hebrews most despised the Roman agents, who they saw as prostitutes. The derogatory term was used to refer to Ezra and the others who sold their bodies for a contract to collect the money they shamelessly handed over to their Roman masters.

"The people, even my neighbors and my relatives, stare at me with anger, and talk behind my back. They curse my name, call me a thief, and spit on the ground after I pass by. And why, I ask, when all I do is collect and record, for their protection, the payments of their taxes?"

This was not a time for spontaneity the Baptist cautioned himself. He thought through his next steps. *This tax collector surprises me. He volunteers a question he knows will generate jeers and loathsome curses, from cowards cloaked in the safety of the crowd. His courage has earned an honest answer. I think I will call him my friend, that will get the crowd's attention.*

"Friend, I respect your courage. You have the honest conviction to say what is on your mind. You do not hide from yourself or attempt to obscure who you are from this crowd," responded the Baptist with care. "As a tax collector your duty is simple, friend. You must never collect more from the subject than is the master's legal share. Not one small coin, can find its way into the Roman treasury, than is required by their code. Nor be skimmed for your personal gain," quickly added the Baptist.

This latest exchange caught the full attention of Gordianus and Calvus. They looked at each other, and shrugged almost in unison, seemingly acknowledging each other's thoughts that the beast was hardly speaking of sedition, resistance or rebellion against Rome. "Gaius will be interested in this," piqued Calvus with subtle irony.

Meanwhile, as the Baptist was engaged with Ezra discussing tribute and taxes, and the Roman soldiers were deciding what and what not would be best to report back to Gaius, a father and his two sons were attempting to hurry by the crowd. Zebadiah was a prosperous merchant, especially skilled in the lucrative but spurious art of money changing. The money changer's tables and stations lined the street that lead directly to the Temple. This usurious activity incensed the Baptist, and when he passed by this gateway to the Temple he would often vomit out of disgust. At these times, he could not suppress or hide the mounting anger and horror that distorted his face and convulsed his body. In this foul state, all the derogatory labels seemed to apply. Here was the desert beast, the water monster, the man eater, the river crocodile, the untamed wild man, the mad ogre, and the dangerous, obsessed zealot on the loose.

"Vile creature," Zebadiah whispered to his sons; Levi the older of the two, and Menashe, still a young man in his teens. He tried to hurry his sons past the crowd while he talked in a hushed voice. "That bearded ogre opens his ugly, toothy mouth and spreads his subversive ideas. He stirs the minds and stokes the fires of hope among the peasant class," cursed Zebadiah.

He warned his sons, "his words are like wine, they fill the heads of peasants and the lower classes with dreams of riches and the foolish notion that the Romans will be vanquished by some shadowy messiah."

"He is a dangerous man. Don't be deceived by all his rough talk about Jehovah's revenge. His real objective, boys, is to spawn a revolution, to cast out the Roman conquerors, and capture all our wealth and redistribute our good fortune among the common dregs and peasants," said Zebadiah hands trembling with anger as he spoke to his sons.

"A curse on his head," said the old man, saliva dripping from his quivering mouth. "That beastly creature rouses spirits to think of insurrection, of ignoring settled law and traditions, and dare to covet and steal our wealth."

"Hold fast to your purses as we pass," the old weasel admonished his pampered sons. "This crowd licks it lips in anticipation. They are drunk from the zealot's words. Their stomachs growl with hunger, and their eyes betray their banal lust to steal our possessions."

As merchants and money changers Zebadiah and his sons were permitted by the Romans to carry small, scabbard knives to protect themselves from would be robbers. Levi and Menashe followed suit with their father and grasped the handles of the sharpened blades that were snugged at their waists with a silk sash. The youthful, immature Menashe, naively quizzed Zebadiah, "but surely, father, Rome will protect us? There are soldiers here. Rome's power is secure. The Legions awesome might could crush this crowd on a moment's notice. Those soldiers are capable of silencing that degenerate creature. They can cut his head off and stop his poisonous ideas from infecting the minds of these low-life peasants."

Levi, not to be left out of the conversation, disdainfully added, "besides, as I see it, these peasants are basically timid cowards. They hear words and dream, but their fear of pain, and suffering and death tie their bodies to their inherited fate. Their lot is set and there they will stay until they die."

Zebadiah nodded in half-hearted agreement with his sons. "True enough, for now. We have Rome's protection, and Rome has no current fear of any Hebrew army casting off its occupation of our country."

"But mark my words, boys; danger lurks wherever poor and squalid creatures find hope and courage through madmen's visions. That incited rabble can rise up and topple temples built of stone, in place a thousand years," warned Zebadiah.

And then it happened; from within the crowd someone shouted above the clamor, "look there," pointing behind the crowd, "see who tries to walk by us unnoticed. Its Zebadiah, the snake, and his serpent sons."

"Cursed day," Zebadiah muttered angrily to his sons, "what evil spirit brought us this way today? We could have taken the eastern route just beyond those hills and no one would have noticed us."

"It was your idea, father, to save a few minutes and come by the river bank," snapped Levi. "Menashe and I wanted to take the longer, safer route to Jerusalem."

"Well, it doesn't matter now; just hurry will you, we need to get to the rise of those hills as quickly as we can. Otherwise, that hideous reptile in the water will have a mob looking to skin our hides," said Zebadiah. The concern in his voice for their safety was not lost on his sons.

The three furtive, well-dressed men were walking quickly at a soldier's fast paced march when, at the sound of the desert beast's sarcastic taunt, they collectively shuddered. "Where do you run to, friends? Why do you hurry from your neighbor's sight? Why such haste? Why not stop and visit," piqued the Baptist?

"If we don't soon get to the other side of that knoll, that mad man will have the mob so angry that they will pick our purses clean and leave our carcasses for the vultures to strip us to our bones," screamed Zebadiah to Levi and Menashe.

"I hope you are right about the Romans, Levi, the soldiers are making their way in our direction. Hurry you slogs, our lives might depend on you," Zebadiah pleaded in quite agony.

Gordianus and Calvus were in no particular hurry, but they would be sure to arrive close by the money changers side in time to stop any real threat of violence. Privately, they enjoyed the fear in the old man's eyes; they, too, had no love for usurers. But they knew if they were late, and physical harm came to Zebadiah, Levi or Menashe, Gaius would have them flogged for dereliction.

Emboldened by the soldiers' arrival, Zebadiah stopped, turned toward the beast, and in fainted respect said: "I am sorry, Baptist. My sons and I have an important meeting with the Governor General in Jerusalem. It would be a serious insult if we were not on time. Otherwise, we would gladly stop and visit with you, and with our good neighbors who are here today."

"Surely, you understand our dilemma," asked Zebadiah. He thought to himself, *holy men never understand the world's ways.* "Perhaps luck will bless us and some other day we can come this way, and stop and chat," said Zebadiah to the Baptist. *Praise God, I will never come this way again, and may I never see your loathsome face for as long as I live,* thought the old man in quiet mockery.

"Oh, I understand Zebadiah," said the Baptist cynically. "Your hands are tied. What else can you do; no doubt your appointment with this important man grows near. We will meet again, I'm sure." *Soon enough old weasel,* the Baptist thought to himself, *you will have another important meeting. You won't be late for that one usurer; and I will guarantee you will receive no more mercy than you show now to your debtors.*

Calvus and Gordianus were relieved that Zebadiah and his sons had moved on without further incident. In their movement toward the ire of the crowd the Roman soldiers had come closer to Mathew's older brother, who stood stoically in place, apparently, content to watch the Baptist from a distance, while keeping close watch over his younger brother.

"Let's play some with the Baptist," Calvus said to Gordianus. Calvus had better command of the Hebrew language than Gordianus, although no one could say he was fluent. In broken Hebrew, Calvus strained to untangle his words, "and what of us, Baptist. What does your Jehovah say? What would you tell a soldier of the Roman Legion?"

The Baptist was no fool, and he realized the dangerous territory he was about to traverse. He took his time. He did his best to measure the impact of each word he was about to utter. "Roman soldiers stand outside of Jewish law and Jehovah's covenant has no bearing on their lives. But, if a Roman soldier does not cheat, or lie, or abuse a prisoner, or murder an innocent person, then Jehovah will not be offended. And, if a Roman soldier shows compassion, grants mercy, and gives alms to the poor and starving, then Jehovah rejoices," answered the Baptist.

The Baptist's clever response left Calvus and Gordianus speechless. They stood in silent ignorance of how to respond. Now they had to worry if and how the incident might be reported to Gaius by others, like the Temple spies. "Damn you, Calvus," said Gordianus, "play with the Baptist you said, but the beast has played us one better." Gordianus let out a sigh of relief when one of the Temple spies, a man named Menach spoke up.

"So, Baptist, now you prophesize to Roman soldiers, as well as the people of Israel," stated Menach. "Your arrogance has no bounds. Soon you will try to preach inside the Holy Temple. Will you dare to instruct the priests on how they should conduct their sacred tasks," asked Menach. "Who are you? Are we to believe you are David's son, do you claim to be the Messiah foretold by old Isaiah?"

His anger heating to boiling point, the Baptist lashed back at Menach. "You Levite snake. You lurk within this lawful gathering, like a snake that hides in the tall grass and waits for some unsuspecting prey to come close enough to bite. What would you have me say?"

"I am not the Messiah, the anointed one," shouted the Baptist. 'Nor am I the savior who will rescue Israel from its oppressors."

"I am only an echo. I am the word of the prophets reborn, that you might hear and understand their vision. I am a voice," said the Baptist, "like the voices of so many prophets who have come before me, who cried out in the wilderness."

With the slightest movement of his eyes the Baptist glanced toward Mathew's older brother and said to the crowd, "Many of you gathered here today, will not die, before God's anointed one, our covenant's Messiah, restores David's kingdom to its glory."

"You say you are not the anointed one," demanded Menach, "then why do you baptize?"

The desert beast's anger had cooled. No longer an erupting volcano, the Baptist had spewed his molten guts. The desert wind and the river current seemed to pause. "I baptize with water from the River Jordon," said the Baptist, "but God's anointed one, Israel's Messiah, will free you with a burst of Jehovah's flaming breath."

Mathew and his older brother had turned and started to walk toward the hillside. Sabella, Miriam and Martha were not far behind as the crowd was breaking up and everyone was going their own way. Calvus and

Gordianus had much to report back to Gaius. It was a strange day and they would discuss the exact details they should share as they marched side by side. Menach would report to Ananias and Caiaphas. He would embellish his involvement to impress the Temple's high priests.

The Baptist made no immediate effort to come ashore. He stood ankle deep in the river and gazed toward the sky. I am finally alone, this is my time, he thought to himself. Now I can talk with Jehovah. *My, God, great creator, and giver of life. My light, my rising sun, my solace. When will my struggle end, Lord? When will you free me from this unbearable burden? When will I no longer have to move among men too timid to stand erect; to speak with people whose ears are plugged; to reason with fools whose minds are too dull to think for themselves, and who lack any vision that rises more than a child's hand above the ground? When, Lord, when will I be free? Have mercy on your weary servant, Lord!*

The Baptist was exhausted. It was late afternoon as he stepped out of the river and walked to a clump of rocks where he laid his pouch, his reed mat and threadbare blanket, and his crooked wooden staff. He slung the pouch with the hemp strap over one shoulder, and then the rolled mat and blanket tied in the middle, it too with a hemp strap, over the other shoulder. He steadied himself with the staff and began his long walk toward the desert. He was exhausted, and it would take several hours to reach a resting place, before the chill of a desert night would settle in and he would rest, fall asleep, and finally be free. In the desert, night approaches quietly. The desert beast slept.

Dreams Beneath an Olive Tree

The morning sun had just begun to dry the moisture that clung to his ebony shaded, textured beard. The desert's night time moisture found resting spaces within its wiry recesses. He slept intermittently that night beneath a scruffy, orphaned olive tree that grew defiantly at the edge of an ancient olive grove. The tree was nestled among the weeds and rocky outcrop. The jutting outcrop gave way to the desert that stretched out below the hilltop grove. He had chosen to rest under the isolated little tree for several reasons. He admired the tree's stubborn determination to insist upon its right to live. A right it claimed despite the obvious neglect its unpruned limbs bore witness to its owner's intentional slight. He also felt a kindred bond, a strange unifying, connecting flux between what he had become—a ragged, weary, isolated traveler—and the solitary, seemingly imperiled olive tree. And finally, he was simply too tired, too physically spent, to climb the hill. He could not muster the energy or resolve to take another step and climb to the higher ground to rest under the grove's lush cluster of flush and manicured olive trees.

This night he and the orphaned tree found comfort, solace and sustenance in each other's company. The exhausted traveler rested his aching back against the tree's sturdy trunk. He stretched his own lanky limbs out over the olive tree's twisted, exposed roots. His chest sagged, as air escaped with a weary sigh. This was his first night away from the desert. He had fled to the desert to avoid the wild talk of the coming of a Jewish Messiah. He was not an acolyte of the messianic prophecies in Hebrew scriptures.

That night, before his eye's heavy lids closed and blocked out the dappled sky, the spent traveler stretched out his arms and with his gnarly hands gently pulled several ripe olives from his evening companion's hanging limbs. The night was still and quiet. The stranger, who stopped for a night's rest, was sure he heard the tree's barely audible gracious invitation to share its fruit. He happily accepted the little tree's offering. He hadn't eaten in nearly three days. His hunger was nearly overwhelming, but he proceeded very slowly. Minutes passed between each welcome bite. He chewed each olive, one at a time, savoring their taste and he thanked his charitable companion for its generosity. He was fortunate, he thought to himself, for the compassion the lonesome tree offered to a weary stranger who passed by and decided to spend the night.

He spoke in a whisper to his new friend, although he had no fear that anyone would overhear his words. There was no one nearby. "Your fruit is ripe, little one. I have never tasted such sweet succulence. You have much to offer, pity it appears your master ignores you. We are so alike in that regard. I, too, feel ignored and maligned. I am alone and miserable. I am so grateful for your company tonight."

What joy a few simple olives bring when your stomach is empty, he thought to himself. *How easily satisfied is the soul of men when stomachs are empty. I have only been three days journey without food and I would sell my robe and sandals for a small loaf of bread and a cup of wine. It's a true tragedy, my generous host. We are so vulnerable; so open to selfishness, mean spiritedness, and depraved, wretched violence, when we want for food, water and shelter. Worse yet are the powerful, wealthy and privileged who hoard more than their share of the bounty of our homeland's gifts to all. Their sin is the greatest. They demean themselves in their greed and are an affront to God for the harm they wreck upon the lives of those who struggle daily just to provide basic needs for their families to survive.*

Again, he broke the silence and spoke out loud to the tree. "Strange, is it not, that I sit hear with you, brother tree. What brought me here other than your hospitality I cannot with any certainty say."

Without waiting for the speechless tree to respond, he continued to reveal his inner thoughts to his captive night-time companion. "What motivated me, what force compelled me, to leave the commune is complicated. It's difficult to explain. Life there was good. We shared what we had; bread, fish, fruit, wine and water. Whatever belonged to one, belonged to all. We prayed to Jehovah and we fasted to purify our bodies, minds and souls. When our bodies and our souls were purged, we replenished ourselves in large group meals, seasoned with conversations that wrestled back and forth regarding God's commandments on our bodies, minds and souls. Then we returned, again, to our ritual practices. The cycle repeated as we prayed and fasted, and then gathered again for food, and water and conversations filled with imagery, and debates of just what holiness entailed."

After a short pause, long enough for the captive, silent tree to respond, he renewed his soliloquy to the passing clouds that occasionally obscured a tiny slice of the starlit sky. "Life was good there, I said this before, brother tree. I know the reasons that I fled. I have an explanation for leaving, but I resist accepting the truth and its consequences. I appear to be doomed whatever might come my way."

"I admit, I was surprised by what Brother Thomas said. Thomas is a member of our commune and quite the skeptic, you see. Anyway, it was his belief that as I slept the Great Tempter entered my unguarded mind, intruded into my dreams and planted a doubting seed inside my skull. Thomas claims the seed germinated and sprouted terrible nightmares that ruin my sleep and leave me exhausted. He claims my efforts to avoid discovering their concealed meaning and coded messages are devouring my soul. But I have a premonition that I will soon discover the meaning and the message, and that will break my fragile spirit and endanger my troubled soul."

"Please take no offense my watchful friend, but at times like this, when I am alone, I often wonder if doubting Thomas is right," the exhausted traveler said to his anchored friend. "I do know, for months now, that as sleep seeks to entwine its protective arms around my weary body, and my mind struggles to drift into refreshing thoughtlessness, sleep comes only in brief interludes. Too often, I am startled and wake in a shivering, cold sweat. In these times, my body convulses in a trembling fear as I see a ferocious river monster tearing flesh from human bones. The monster devours all who dare approach the water that he haunts. He ravages my brothers and my sisters and imperils our race. Their floating skeletons, stripped of flesh, haunt my dreams. Worse yet, the visions now intrude into the day. I see the terrible consuming beast throughout the day. I cannot close my mind or shut my eyes. I can't escape; all day, all night I obsess about the river monster my dreams have unleashed."

Sleep will not come easily this night, he thought in restless silence. "It is there, little friend, every night in my dreams. It bellows, growls, hisses and snaps its teeth in the air. Then it changes tactics. Its voice, soft as a lovers entreat, beckons, urges, cajoles, and tries seductively to draw me closer to the river's edge. But I always see its glowing, hideous red eyes. They stare at me, pulling me ever closer to the brown murky water it inhabits. Always, I resist. I drag my feet. I grab hold of a rocky outcrop or a tree, like you my little brother, and I hold on."

Imploringly he called out, no longer afraid that he might be overheard. "Perhaps tonight I will need to grasp your sturdy trunk, little brother. Be ready my new-found friend, I may need your courage and your help. For I have a real foreboding, a frightening dread. I will be lost if I am pulled into that river. Surely, then, that unrelenting beast will devour a wooden-headed carpenter such as me."

His conversation with the little olive tree trailed off as his drooping eye lids finally closed. At last, he gave up his stubborn opposition to sleep's unrelenting demand. His mind's conscious resistance gave way to his exhausted body's vain attempt to thwart sleep's imminent ascendance and control. But the respite was brief. And then, beneath the olive tree, it happened as it did every night. The dreams, no longer held in check by the mind's conscious defenses, cascaded from one ominous waterfall to another.

"Wake up carpenter, this is no time to sleep," an angry voiced called out.

"It's your turn. I have done my duty, now it is your turn to advance Jehovah's cause. It's your responsibility to carry his people farther up the summit," the protagonist's voice called out.

"You are the one who now must bear God's burden on your shoulders. I'm finished. Now you must find the route that I failed to discover. There is a hidden passage that opens the ascending path to God. I could not find it, but you must."

He spoke in a tone of mournful pity for the man he intended to curse, passing along a burden he could no longer endure. "I'm sorry, but I could not inspire others to simply take the first necessary step and stretch out their hands to God. I preached that God in turn would reach across time's abyss to touch their troubled souls and show them the ascending path. Sadly, tragically, they stood in silence and failed to act. I did my best but I have failed.

"There is no hiding from that truth; there is no mercy for my nonfeasance," the dream robber said somberly.

"Don't pretend you are asleep and that you don't hear me carpenter," the sleep robber shrieked.

"I am alive in your twisted dream and you know I speak the truth. You are no fool. You like to call yourself 'wooden head' but you are sly. Your head is not as hard as the wood that you once used to build doors and shutters for villager's homes. You were a carpenter flush with work before you fled to that foolish commune."

"What possessed you to join that group of escapist misfits who searched for God within a cloistered community," he asked the startled carpenter who could not determine if he was awake or still asleep.

"I saw you retreat from reality. You and your reclusive friends who tried to hide from this world's pain and suffering. You foolishly tried to blot out the disgrace of occupation and stifling oppression. You turned your back to the corruption and deceit that plagues the Temple priests. And, worst of all, you ignored the basic needs and yearning for freedom, comfort and happiness that alludes your race."

"Look at me," the nightmare caller demanded. "You must become freedom's instrument for all of Israel's people."

With a sinister sneer, the wild thing who horrified the carpenter, and who recurrently appeared as a terrifying river monster in his nightmarish dreams, kept up his relentless assault. "Your anguished people call out. You can no longer run and hide from them or me. I will haunt your dreams until you rise beyond yourself and take on your people's burden. You will not be free until you free your race of the ominous yoke that renders men weak slaves; that turns them into cowards afraid to behave honorably, let alone act heroically."

The carpenter learned his trade from his father. He inherited the family business after his father died. No one would call them prosperous, but the work was steady and provided sufficient support to meet their family's basic needs. They were both hard workers, the father and the eldest son. Their bodies were lean, but their frames were ribbed with sinewy muscle. No one would call the young carpenter a giant, but he was a large, formidable looking young man. Father and son both gained their physical strength from laboring hour after hour, working with heavy wood that they planed laboriously into planks and then cut and sized for window shutters and threshold doors for village homes.

One day while they were taking a break from their work, seated on the ground resting during the mid-day heat, his father grasped his chest and died. The elder carpenter passed away before he had time to utter a single word. After his father's death, the young carpenter lived with and supported his mother, Miriam, sister, Martha, and younger brother Mathew.

He was a good craftsman. His father had trained him well. He learned the wood worker's craft easily. But his father also made sure that his precocious son learned to read and write Hebrew. His father had an intuitive grasp that there was more in store for his son than the life of a simple carpenter. Unlike his father, the young carpenter was a prolific conversationalist and an excellent story teller. He was a bit slow in completing his contracted work because he would often engage in lengthy conversations with any passerby who stopped to admire his handiwork. People tolerated his rather lackadaisical pace on task because the quality of his work was well known and not easily replicated elsewhere. But many village residents, not all who were customers, enjoyed the carpenter's vivid descriptions of and novel insights into the Jewish scriptures and traditions. The entertaining stories seemed to pour out of his mouth spontaneously whenever he took a break from his work and people were nearby. The carpenter-philosopher was gaining a reputation as a wise, compassionate, holy man. He was quick to dismiss any such rumors. Despite his disavowal, the rumors had begun to reach the attention of the Temple priests and the Roman occupying force commanders. The Jewish Sanhedrin and the Roman Legion were well positioned with spies in the community and within their own organizations. Trust was a rare commodity those days and suspicion took root everywhere.

He was a young man when his father died. He was the head of the household for many years because of his father's early death. He willingly took on the responsibility of providing for his mother Miriam, sister Martha, and younger brother Mathew. Mathew never mastered the carpenter's trade, other than its rudiments. Mathew was too young at the time to do any significant work in their small shop. Because of this, he often secured his father's permission, and later his older brother's agreement, to help the fisherman who worked the nearby Sea of Galilee.

The carpenter was devoted to his family's care and well-being. Although he was fond of and attracted to Sabella, Martha's good friend, he did not see how he could take on the added responsibility of marriage and support a family beyond his widowed mother, and unmarried sister and younger brother. After all, he would reason with himself, he was the eldest son and they were all justifiably dependent on him. He thought his time would come. He hoped, silently to himself, that Sabella would be able to wait until he had the opportunity to propose marriage, and to celebrate an ancient rite he felt was already too long delayed.

That he was fond of Sabella was obvious. There was a visible chemistry between the carpenter and Sabella. Whenever she would visit Martha at their home, the carpenter always seemed to be around. Sabella was hauntingly beautiful. She had the dark complexion of her ancient Jewish Bedouin stock. Her hair was so black it almost appeared velvet as it peered out from her head scarf. She had subtle features other than her eyes. Her eyes, hazel with green speckles, were distinctive, unforgettable, and to some utterly unnerving. They were so unlike what you might expect from someone otherwise so Mediterranean in appearance. It was hard not to gaze at her eyes, and the carpenter would often become embarrassed when he suddenly realized he had been staring into her eyes longer than convention would consider polite. Despite their attempts to hide their playful flirtatious interactions, the carpenter always stopped short of saying how fond he was of Sabella. His sense of duty to his family always intruded and he would hold his tongue in check.

"I'm back carpenter," the night monster asserted himself. "You can't hide from me. I know you want to run from me. I know I am not a welcome visitor in your sleep. You dread seeing me and you despise hearing my voice in your dreams. But you are my prey, and I have you in my grasp. You cannot escape me or your duty to your race."

"Leave me be; you are disgusting, ogre!" the carpenter shouted back to the apparition he decried as the dream thief.

"Go find someone else to torment. I am no savior for my race," the carpenter implored.

"I was once a happy man. I had a trade. I worked with wood. I cared for my family. I had friends and strangers who visited or just stopped by and enjoyed my stories. We had delightful conversations."

"And damn you," the carpenter lashed out angrily at his tormentor, "I had the prospect of love and a normal life. It was only a matter of time before my sister and younger brother were married and on their own. And then, Sabella and I would be free to marry, to have children, to work my trade, and to live out our lives in simple comfort and happiness."

The carpenter paused, stared at the dream thief, and sighed. "That was until you robbed me of my dreams with your taunting, nightmarish, relentless mind games."

"I was not inclined to join the Essenes. Certainly, not before you stole my peace and happiness, before you raped my dreams, before you stole my expectations for a normal life. I gave up all I had, all I loved, to run from you. Yes, beast, I sought safety in the brotherhood of that commune," the carpenter shouted at his tormentor.

"But then, they, too, sought to push me to be something I was not," said the carpenter with resignation in his voice.

"I fled from my brethren, my brothers and sisters of the commune just as I have been fleeing from you, tormentor. I fled to the desert, to solitude." The carpenter's mouth was dry from talking and he tried to spit at the feet of his persecutor. But his tormentor seemed imperious to the insult, and the carpenter's constant rebuffs.

"I have told you, and I told them, until my throat was dry and parched, that I am not the savior of my race. I am not their imaginary promised heir to King David's long-lost throne. I am not a wise holy man whose wisdom and words bring comfort and hope to my race."

"You're all fools," he winced. "I abandoned my own family. I abandoned the Essenes. I abandoned reason and hope to wander in the desert the past forty days. I'm a commonplace, failed, human with a tormented mind and very ordinary soul. There is nothing about me that is extraordinary, let alone divine as some fools would like to believe."

The carpenter shook his head back and forth. "It's a lie. It's a pack of lies. I'm a story teller, nothing more. And now that gift has become a curse, a death shroud to any hope I ever had for a peaceful life and happiness."

"It's your fault. And now you have a deluded ally in that desert beast, John, the firebrand Baptist. I'm aware how he haunts the Jordan River banks like you haunt my dreams. He fills people's minds with dribble about some fantasized Messiah who will come and magically throw off the Roman occupation and restore Israel's glorious past," the carpenter said in mocking disgust.

Piqued, the dream haunter said in a retort, "and your point is what, carpenter?"

"Why do you keep tormenting me? You're bad enough, now you bring that Wildman into my dreams. The Baptist is real. He isn't a figment of my disturbed sleep, like you. He has followers and he has detractors. Some people tremble with fear hearing his wild claims that he is a prophet who has God's ear. Others are agitated and annoyed, even alarmed, with his incessant preaching about the emergence of a savior for Israel; a divine intervener," the Carpenter said mockingly.

"Mathew, my younger brother, is infected with this savior talk. It's gibberish," the carpenter exclaimed.

"I fled the commune because two of my friends, former fishermen, Aaron and Harel were calling me Teacher. They were trying to persuade others among our Essene brethren that I was a holy man; that I was Jehovah's long delayed Messiah."

"I told them to stop. I said it's wizardry; stop the blasphemy before you are banished from the commune, I pleaded with them."

"In the end, I had to flee the commune. I had to silence them. They had to stop spreading their false hopes that a wooden-headed carpenter, who likes people and enjoys telling stories, was somehow Israel's promised savior. However well-intended they thought they were, they were sowing the seeds of their destruction. They were placing themselves and their families in grave danger. The corrupt Temple priests and the brutal Roman legionnaires were taking notice. Soon, in their self-interests, alone or conspiring, forces of power and control would scorch the earth to rid Israel of what they would call a deadly pestilence," the carpenter declared.

"Go back to the river. Please leave me alone, beast," the Carpenter pleaded.

"Go torment the Baptist. You sound alike. You look alike. You could be brothers. Go convince him to save our race," the carpenter implored.

Night moved on slowly. The moon was in no hurry to permit her daytime challenger an early arrival. For the moment, night would hold sway. The carpenter's mind was temporarily free of its tormentor. His body had insisted upon its necessary claim for rest. Sleep was essential and the poor, tormented carpenter would expire from exhaustion if his sleep was further delayed. Sleep came, but so too his unwanted dreams.

"I'm back, carpenter. I told you it is fruitless to try to run and hide from me. I will not leave your dreams or your daily thoughts until you head my words. It is now your duty, your responsibility, your burden to lead your people up the steep and craggy ascent to that higher spiritual plane where Jehovah resides. That is your inescapable solemn duty to your race," the tormentor said, interrupting once again the carpenter's valiant but vain attempt to flee from his nemesis, if only in his sleep.

"Be gone beast," the carpenter responded angrily, his brief interlude of sleep disturbed by the relentless return of his dreams' recurrent tormentor. "You push and drag me constantly toward death's door. It's you I flee from and fear."

"Not so, carpenter. It is your conscience and your imperiled mind that compels you to flee, not me," the sleep depriver said sarcastically.

"We both know why you fled your family and left behind your carpenter shop, don't we carpenter," the tormentor asked his frazzled prey.

"For a while, carpenter, it was enough for you to talk with your customers and the growing numbers of passersby's. It was safe for you to condemn the injustice and cruelty of the Roman crucifixions of your Jewish brothers. You challenged the veracity of the charges of sedition and plots of armed rebellion. But then carpenter, you were confronted with a moral choice, and rather than confront the Roman soldiers, you abandoned your family and fled."

"Not so! You are a disgusting, odious beast," screamed the carpenter.

"I refused to build the damned beams the Romans wanted for their vile crucifixions. I made a moral choice, I followed my conscience and the right path. Yes, I spared myself imprisonment and probably a crucifying death, but I also spared my family from inevitable harassment and likely harm," the carpenter sneered at his tormenter.

"You say, I fled to the Essenes. But you are wrong. I acted. I did not acquiesce. I was not complicit with the brutal Roman forces that persecute my race. I defied them, you addle minded fiend," shouted the carpenter.

"I chose the right path to protect my family and to avoid being a collaborator. In fleeing to the peaceful, sequestered Essenes, as you mockingly allege, the Romans concluded I was a harmless religious fanatic that posed no threat. The Sanhedrin was glad to see potential dissidents retreat from the city and set up peace loving communities in the countryside. I left because I knew the Romans would continue their pogrom and their crucifixions, and the murderers would find another collaborator to build their crucifixion beams. My family and I have escaped retaliation. How difficult is that to understand," the carpenter bitterly asked his adversary.

The antagonist imbedded in his head was silent for the moment, held in check within the carpenter's unfolding dream.

"You also say I fled from the Essenes, and you are right. But what you overlook, monster in my dreams, is that I fled for the sake of my brothers and my sisters in the commune, not for myself," the carpenter explained.

"No one paid attention to the Essenes until my brother, Mathew, and his well-intentioned but misguided friends, Aaron and Harel, began to talk, at first quietly and then more openly. They spread gibberish that I was a holy man, a teacher, perhaps even the mad Baptist's prophesized Messiah."

The carpenter moved his head, insultingly spat on the ground, and looked directly at the glowing eyes of his tormentor. "When religious zealots like that Baptist stir the cooking pot with ideas of a restored Jewish kingdom, and normally withdrawn cloistered communities start rumors that one of their own is showing signs of divinity, that is when authorities—religious and political—begin to fear their status quo is in jeopardy. Paranoia soon follows, the spies are deployed, and no one escapes suspicion and unjustified scrutiny. That, dream robber, is what led me to the desert these past forty days," said the carpenter as he extended a hand and pointed a finger directly at the specter that haunted his dreams.

"I had no illusions, and my desert pilgrimage confirmed for me, once and for all that I have no claim to divinity. I spoke to Jehovah every day I wandered in the desert to the point I was delirious and close to expiring. And did Jehovah speak to me? No, beast. Not once. God was silent, and I was rebuked."

"I'm a carpenter. I want to be a carpenter. I want to live a normal life. Why is that so hard for others to understand? Why don't you understand," asked the carpenter imploringly?

"Precisely, carpenter," his tormentor replied. "I never said you were divine. I only said it was your duty to take on the mantle of your oppressed race and march them higher up the summit toward Jehovah and his outreached hand."

"It would defeat the purpose of the prophesy of a Messiah, if Israel's liberator was divine." The dream ghost's face crinkled with a slight squinch as it peered back at the carpenter and said, "but you already know this, don't you carpenter? You understand this far better than the whole Essene commune, and the Baptist and his few beleaguered followers."

The carpenter did not respond but the dream intruder would not let its assertion pass by. "The Messiah has to be mortal. The liberator must be a human. Only a man can take on this burden, carry on the struggle, and make the sacrifices required to save his race. For what would it prove, what would it demonstrate to ordinary men and women, if the Messiah was Jehovah's son come to save the Jews? Such a heavenly soul would be invincible, incapable of entering death's trap door. There would be no sacrifice in this, only a temporary inconvenience."

"No, carpenter," the tormentor said with conviction, "only a man can heroically take on the pain and suffering, and death too if that is the cost, to lead Jehovah's people to that higher spiritual plane. It is a human, not a god that this Messiah must be. What would Jehovah care if his son led Israel's people up the mountain summit? What does it prove if a god saves the world and dies in the process, only to live forever because of its divine nature? It only matters to Jehovah if a mortal man accepts the call to sacrifice and struggle. It's a man that must find that summit passage, and take our besieged race to the peak where God resides. You, carpenter, must carry your race up through the cold, thin air, where your people will finally be in a place pure enough, in thought and in action, to touch God's outstretched hand. Their salvation is in your hands, and your salvation depends upon their salvation."

The carpenter was jarred from his fitful sleep as his tormentor vanished like a vapor, but not before he heard the dream ghost boast, "it's you, carpenter! You can no longer run and hide from the truth, you are Jehovah's instrument of delivery for your race. You are the Liberator. Now wake up, get on your feet and go confront the Baptist who is the real river monster of your dreams."

Sharing Tea

IT WAS THE SEASON of Ramadan, the ninth month of the Muslim year, a time of daily fasting that begins when the first hint of daylight, hidden by its nocturnal sibling rival—night, pokes its slowly awakening head above the eastern horizon. The faithful languish in their abstention throughout the day while the twin brothers—sun and daylight—retreat fully west, threading their way toward a glance of their sisters—moon and night. The fast ends, and appetites are sated with nightly feasts as the twin brothers pass below the western horizon and vanish from sight, giving birth again to their sister, the moon, who rises to ascendance in the splendor of the nocturnal night.

In Libya, Ramadan is often called "the hot month." But the young American airman who had leapt from the rear of a flatbed military troop transport placed no special significance on this folksy notion concerning Ramadan season. It was clear to him, based upon his experience, it's always scorching hot in Libya. There was no escape from the sun and its penetrating heat.

On this day, too, the sun shone unmercifully upon the sandy, sparsely vegetated North African landscape. The intense, angry heat came oven-like from the sun's bold glaring face and rarely subsided until long after daylight was wrestled into submission by its rival sister—night. Each day the warring siblings battle for ascendance. Always one retreats and the other ascends to prominence, only to fall as its returning sibling, refreshed from its labors of dominance, reasserts itself and the process begins anew.

Michael Robert Welch brushed grains of clinging sand off the seat of his olive drab military fatigues (this was 1967, long before the U. S. wars in the middle east and the advent of sandstone color camouflaged fatigues). He gave a slight tug on a leather leash secured around his wrist, while at the other end the other member of this sentry dog team, Ajax, turned his head in a slight but respectful nod toward Sergeant Welch. Meanwhile, Hamad Mohamed, like Welch with three stripe chevrons on his sleeves, alighted from the troop transport carrier moments later. Hamad's canine partner, Bruno, lumbered out behind him.

Both animals were large. Bruno was immense for a German Shepherd bred, at 29 inches at the withers (three inches taller than to expect) and weighing a full 125 pounds. Ajax, at 90 pounds and normal height, was an even more formidable specimen. He brandished a large broad forehead and thick mane of hair that gave him the appearance, not of a distant Canis lupus relative, more a young, small-maned male lion on the prowl. The U.S. Air Force Military Police Canine Corps kennel at Wheelus Air Base housed 120 sentry dogs that came in an array of sizes and coat colors that simply challenged bred standards and spoke to an amazing diversity within the bred. All but two were male; all of course neutered or spayed.

In theory, and most often in practice, the human member of these teams was the alpha figure, but sometimes the handlers questioned whether it was man or dog that decided what route on patrol the team would take, what steps were next. This was the question most acute in the handler's minds when one of the powerful, alert and vigilant dogs became immediately alert and visibly agitated by an inattentive passing rabbit or fox.

The two men, with their dogs muzzled and sitting by their sides watched the troop transport pull away from the drop spot located just outside the main gate to the stone walled enclosure that surrounded and protected Skadada Wells. The well and pump station located several miles off the twenty-square mile military installation that in the late 60's housed up to fifteen thousand U.S. military, civilians, and dependents, was one of two such facilities that drew water from the coastal aquifer that was the main water source sustaining the base. The wall was nearly ten feet tall at the top of the stone. Broken pieces of glass were embedded in cement on the top layer of stone, and this imposing obstacle was crowned with a foot of barbed wire. The wall was not a product of American ingenuity or harshness, it was in fact a vestige of the 1911 to 1947 Italian colonization and military occupation of Libya.

But this was 1967, still before the June 1967 Six-Day War when Israel took a preemptive strike at Egypt and destroyed Egypt's air force and captured additional territory in the Sinai desert, the Golan Heights and Gaza Strip, and security, not as vigilant as it would become, was somewhat taken for granted. In truth, the wall itself was not impenetrable. It was the large, malevolent looking dogs and equally unsettling armed sentries that stopped any uninvited intruder from venturing into this wolf's den. If water is the sustaining source of life, Skadada Wells was the life blood of Wheelus Air Base.

Born on different continents, in different generations (Hamad was 20 years Michael's senior), in distinctive and at times alien cultures, the two men resembled each other more closely than did their paper-pedigreed, pure breed dogs, whose species was the product of hundreds of years of selective breeding. Hamad was an inch shorter than Michael and his complexion appeared darker than Michaels, but the actual difference was Hamad's less freshly shaved thicker beard. The shadow of a second day growth on Hamad's face belied the fact that Michael's complexion was no fairer.

Hamad extended his right arm and pointed to the retreating sun which still had an hour's journey before it would drop below the horizon and signal an end to a Muslim's daily fasting. "We can make our patrol rounds, return to the pump station building, and then, praise be to Allah, share a bite of food."

"Is that alright with you, Michael" entreated Hamad as he smiled at his good fortune. The height of the wall would expedite the sun's retreating path below the horizon and give Hamad a head-start on his preparations for their evening meal.

Hamad had come prepared for a small feast, certainly appropriate in view of a day's sacrifice of fasting. His World War Two vintage tawny colored nap sack was loaded with several small loaves of flat bread baked earlier in the morning, several small plastic sandwich bags separately filled with olives and grapes, and a plastic container with small cubed pieces of camel meat secured that morning from the open market butcher's shop. If he hurried through his patrol of the center area of the grounds, Hamad was self-assured he would be able to finish his rounds in time for prayers, to start a fire, skewer the meat cubes on a spit, boil water for tea, and watch the final rays of sunlight disappear below the wall before Michael returned from his longer patrol route along the inside perimeter of the enclosure.

"See you in an hour, Hamad," said Michael, as he removed the muzzle from Ajax's head, and together, they started a leisurely paced walk around the roughly 100-acre site.He and Ajax would walk at a slow pace, stopping along the way for the dog to sniff, raise his leg, and mark his territory a half-dozen times along the way,

"Try to be back by sundown, please," entreated Hamad.

"Sure, Hamad," Michael replied. "Have I ever been late for a meal that breaks a Ramadan fast?" Hamad just rolled his eyes in mild amusement.

Michael could see the bright orange and yellow flames of the fire from several hundred yards away as he made his way back to the main pump building. The flames danced in ascending spirals, easily visible against the background of approaching darkness. Michael could hear the crackle of the burning wood and smell the skewered meat cubes sizzling on the turning spit as he approached the circular brick cooking pit the Libyan guards had constructed out of a pile of old bricks left near the rear of the main pump station building, probably left behind as surplus from the original building site decades ago.

"I was beginning to think the evening meal was going to start without you," Hamad said with a trace of annoyance in his voice.

Then Hamad said in a softer conciliatory tone, "it's time for prayer."

Michael did not join his Muslim friend in evening prayer. Michael was not a Muslim or even a religious man. He just sat quietly out of respect, and in silence stared at his Libyan companion who was seated on the ground hardly an arm's length from the fire's darting flames. Hamad bowed toward Mecca and rhythmically intoned the evening prayer that God is Great.

When Hamad finished prayers, he said to Michael, "please tie your dog's leash to that bush so that we can share this meal." Hamad said this somewhat imploringly, he was after all hungry, nodding his head toward a short bristly thistle shrub not far from the corner of the pump station building.

Michael returned and found a canteen plate full of several cubes of wood grilled meat and a handful of olives, topped off with a small, flat, piece of bread torn from one of the circular loaves.

"Thank you, Hamad, it is really kind of you to share this food with me. Unlike you I haven't fasted, although I haven't eaten much. I just feel down today."

"What do you mean, are you ill, are you sad? I don't understand what you are saying," responded Hamad.

Michael smiled on the inside trying to keep his little amusement to himself and said, "depressed Hamad. I feel sad and troubled today."

Although there was no disputing that Hamad's mastery of English was far superior to Michael's cursory grasp of Arabic, Michael was privately amused that Hamad did not seem to understand the English colloquialism in his use of the word "down". The smile faded as he realized there had to be thousands of nuances in Arabic that were beyond any possible understanding on his part.

Hamad had consumed most of the olives on his tarnished metal plate. The remaining bread lay to the side in crescent shape. He finished chewing and swallowed his second meat cube, and then with a short motion of his right arm Hamad wiped away some vestige of grease from his lips. The residue was transferred to a sleeve of his uniform jacket.

"Please eat the meat while it is still warm. When you are done, we can enjoy some grapes and a glass of *shay*, and then we can talk about what troubles you," said Hamad.

Michael smiled, he too, preferred to use the Arabic word *shay* to refer to tea (tea in Arabic was pronounced like "shay-he," placing emphasis on a strong *e* at the end).

Michael slowly chewed the meat. This was not the first time he had eaten camel. He found the meat tasty. Once he overcame his initial aversion to the idea of eating camel, he rarely turned down a meal involving the ugly humped animal. The meat was more course than beef, but he imagined his friends back home in Michigan who called him Bobby, would never know the difference between barbecued beef or camel shish-kebabs unless they were told so after they had eaten. He knew that most would never be adventuresome enough to eat the foreign meat, never if they were told what it was in advance.

Night had fully arrived. Clouds shrouded the ground in a blanket of darkness. The stars were in hiding, hidden safely behind a thick cover of clouds, and neither Michael or Hamad, from their vantage point below could discern the moon's flirtatious dance with heaven's fire flies. Only the ebbing flames of the cooking pit cut through the darkness of the night, and mapped out the silhouettes of the two men seated around the fire.

Although the daytime in Libya was stifling, the damp night air in Tripoli that drifted inland from the near-by Mediterranean Sea (Wheelus Air Base had a long stretch of beach on its northern limits) had a cool edge that chilled the blood thin limbs of anyone who had become acclimated to its climate.

"I will never understand how it can be so hot during the day and turn so cold at night," Michael observed as he tossed the last three branches of wood, that Hamad had gathered earlier, into the cooking pit.

The wood rekindled the fire and flames leapt skyward as Hamad removed the small metal tea pot that had dangled from the spit's cross rail.

The tea had been brewing from the moment Hamad first lit a match to start the fire.

"How about some *shay*, Michael" Hamad asked as he extended a small glass of the skillfully brewed tea to toward his friend.

Michael was especially fond of the way Libyans prepared *shay*. The tea was brewed in a small tea pot for a very long time. Sugar was heaped periodically into the boiling cauldron and then the thick liquid was poured into small glasses just like the ones you see bartenders, in any local bar, use for shots of liquor. Peanuts, just several to a glass, were added into the *shay* when available and the finished product was sipped as a connoisseur might gently nurse an aged single malt scotch whiskey, or a sommelier at a well-known California restaurant would sniff and sip an exquisite Napa Valley merlot.

Hamad placed his glass of *shay* on one of the cooking pit's bricks. The savory *shay* was too delightful to hastily consume. Good things are not for rushing. Hamad studied his American companion. The two often worked Skadada Wells together but Hamad could not recall another time when Michael seemed so distracted, so distant.

Hamad asked, "Well Michael, what is it that troubles you tonight? You are here, and yet, you are not here. Are you thinking of home?"

Michael shrugged his shoulders ever slightly saying no. "Well, yes, in a way I guess that I am," said Michael vacillating.

"Do your parents remain in good health?" inquired Hamad.

"Oh yes, Hamad, my parents are fine, but I have not heard from Mary Elizabeth for several weeks, not single letter or card. I fear the worst is coming," said Michael, not able to hide the pained expression on his face. Why else wouldn't she write he thought to himself.

Hamad stared at Michael for a moment without responding. Despite the dark night and the waning fire, the suffering and pain that Michael was projecting could not hide from anyone other than a most obtuse observer.

"She doesn't know how to tell me, Hamad. She can't find words that work for her to put her feelings down on paper."

"Tell you what, Michael," Hamad gently asked with some foreboding of what was to come.

"That it's over between us," he responded.

Painfully he proceeded, "she has found someone else to love, Hamad. I can feel it. Someone who is there, back home, there for her now. Someone real, not a photograph, not a memory from the past. She has someone else, someone she can see, reach out and touch, someone to hold right now and not wait for endless months for me to finish here and then go to my next base, probably to Vietnam."

"Michael, your mind races to conclusions. You speculate too much. It's not as though you have vanished from her life. You are not the Mediterranean fog that disappears into the bright heat of my Libya's morning sun," answered Hamad.

"It may be true that in this moment, you are not there, and you cannot embrace, not flesh to flesh. But you are not some feckless cloud. You are flesh and bone. You have substance. You are alive. You still share this time with your love. In Allah's mercy, it does not matter that you do not share this place, this spot of earth at this precise moment," entreated Hamad, who with all the compassion he could summon reached out with empathy and grasped Michael's hand in his.

With some inclination of what Michael would say Hamad asked Michael if he still loved his Mary Beth, and as anticipated Michael with a little irritation responded, "Yes, of course I do."

"Well then," said Hamad, "time and place are irrelevant."

Michael looked hard at Hamad's face. He thought to himself, *well that is not in the Quran*, but out of friendship and respect for others' religions said nothing. He also thought, again to himself, how profound his friend's insights always seemed to be.

"Don't you see, Michael? Love is our window into eternity. Once given, it cannot be taken back. You gave it freely Michael, it was spent the moment it was given," Hamad said with genuine sentiment.

The sound of the charred wood crackling in the throes of the fire's last urgings went unnoticed, as Michael shifted all his attention to his friend's deep personal insights into love and life.

"Love is man's bridge over the abyss. It is our only path to the eternal, Michael. We do not know, nor have another way to reach paradise," Hamad said empathically.

With passion rising in his voice, Hamad, in an elevated pitch went on. "Warrior. Patriot. Mystic. Parent. Hero. Lover. There is no difference, all is sacrifice."

"My grandfather, who even now twenty years since he died sends an occasional chill to my spine, said to me when I was just a small boy that human nobility is entwined in sacrifice, and sacrifice, in its most refined expression, is love," said Hamad hoping that he had not disturbed his Bedouin-warrior grandfather from his well-deserved eternal rest.

Hamad always implored Allah, and prayed in silent dread: *May his rest not be disturbed when I dare to use his name and repeat words that the old man himself once used;* words designed to help his struggling grandson open his own mind to what too often seemed to be intractable contradictions in the daily challenges of survival and the search for happiness.

And then continuing, Hamad said to Michael. "A few years later while I was left alone for a month at my grandfather's tent; this was, I think the day after he had buried his beloved wife, my grandmother, the old man said to me; "Hamad, when we love another human being, out of necessity we give to that person a part of our very own soul. And that part of our soul—that part that we sacrifice and freely give is an act of love—we relinquish it and its recipient does not have Allah's good grace to ever return that gift to its giver. In sacrifice, like in battle when we lose a limb, we forfeit that part of our soul. It is given in sacrifice and love and it remains, that part of our soul, with the object of our love forever."

"You see, Michael," Hamad continued almost non-stop, "it is as if two great sand storms collide. They merge, intertwine and blend, and then continue their separate tracks. They remain fundamentally the same, however, they too are altered and take with them some of the sand from the other storm." Easing the pressure on Michael's hand, Hamad held on briefly in reassurance and the promise of hope.

"You must realize that your love for your girlfriend is no less real because time or place separate you. Your love is a gift that she takes with her because you have given it to her."

"Yesterday. Today. Tomorrow. It simply does not matter when or if she draws upon your love or not. What matters is that you have given her the gift of love, and hopefully you can draw upon the love that she too gave to you as her gift. If it is truly love that you exchanged, then you have given to each other parts of your souls. Like the sandstorms your souls retain the elements exchanged," said Hamad.

"Michael," Hamad continued, "she will take that part of your soul—your gifted love—wherever she goes for the breadth of her life's journey. And so, too, her gifted love travels with you."

Michael understood and felt the import of what Hamad had said, but his heart remained heavy. Hamad, always a compassionate soul (a misfit in the army in some regards, until he had to summon his grandfather's fierce tribal traits and physical action was demanded), was not ready to leave Michael suffering on his own.

"Michael, I would like to tell you a story. Would you mind," asked Hamad.

"Hamad, you have done much more than any friend I know could do to ease my pain," replied Michael.

"But no, go ahead, especially if you plan to resurrect your grandfather for another of his wondrous tales."

Hamad was a splendid story teller and Michael never tired of conversations while Hamad shared adventures sourced back to his grandfather. The stories were rich in dialogue and detail and always had a mythic and heroic theme.

"Why yes, of course, who else", said Hamad barely able to contain a grin. Hamad loved his grandfather in the way an unsure child admires a beast that looms just out of harm's way, and leaves the child's mind free to play in safe distance from wild, savage, untamed things.

Hamad's grandfather was a paradox. As a child, Hamad would tremble and turn away if his gaze lingered too long into his grandfather's rare steel grey eyes; eyes that Hamad thought belonged in a wolf's den not in the spacious tent his grandmother made into a safe, welcoming space. To this day, when Hamad would begin to embellish a tale that his grandfather once told him, he would stop and immediately say a silent prayer to Allah. He would plead that his grandfather would not be disturbed from his sleep, and alerted, see his grandson with those haunting eyes that seemed to Hamad as sharp and cold as the steel blade of the old Bedouin's scabbarded curved knife. To Hamad the old man seemed always on the ready to withdraw the knife to defend himself or to correct some knave's insult to a member of his extended clan. The old man was truly rooted in the behavior of his ancient relatives who looked with distrust on every word, practice, behavior and person not within the blood line of their tribal clans. It did not strike Michael as odd that Hamad, a man whose status (best Michael could determine) was obtained through blood trails back to his grandfather's tribal clan, was a paradox as well. Hamad was not a university educated man, and yet he often displayed the intellect of a genius, the intuition of a seer, and the compassion of a saint.

And so, for the next hour Hamad resurrected a tale of pain, sacrifice and love that his grandfather had shared with his adolescent grandson while they sat side by side on the ground at the entrance to the old goat herder and tribal leader's tent.

"I remember, like it was yesterday Michael," said Hamad, "the story of a hidden scroll and Fatima, a girl, and a boy named Kahlil." Michael listened with trance-like attention as Hamad recast a story that shaped his life from that day forward.

Kahlil and Fatima were members of a Bedouin tribe, each belonging to a different clan. The two clans, lived as one tribe, herding sheep and goats, and watching over their traveling companion camels. Their way of life was nomadic with roots that reached back to biblical times. They eschewed the larger more populated areas of settlement that developed nearer coastal areas where water, food and commerce were historically more easily obtained. But the clans were steeped with hardy, resolute people and flourished in modest terms until together the tribe had outgrown survival size, and the essence of their way of life was in jeopardy. This was a moral crisis that the tribal leaders had to address, and so the leaders within the clans gathered at a tribal council around a communal fire to debate what course to take; to find a solution that would protect and continue their chosen way of life.

Hamad spent time explaining how a young girl, Fatima, and a young boy, Kahlil, had been bartered to each other (along with a collection of animals and thatched mats) to marry once passage through adolescence was achieved. Brokered marriages among these nomadic people were a form of clan and tribal survival, protecting against the bane of incest and avoiding jealous adolescent rivalry and feuds. But the two, who often moved together herding the clans' collection of goats and sheep, seemed to have a sense of attraction outside their parental pledges of future fidelity. They glimpsed in each other's eyes the kindling of affection. And so, only months since adolescence's first breach, the girl and boy watched from safe distance the debate that raged among the clans' elders on what best represented the tribe's chances to survive.

The two clans had agreed that rumors of better grazing lands, and good springs of flowing water and fuller wells, were worth the risk of a perilous journey to a better land. But that was where the agreement stopped. What was left was a bitter unresolved difference in what route was best to take. And so, a compromise was struck, the clans would travel together the first years of their trek; then they would split off and travel separate paths, each along some ancient caravan route, and each laden with different perils and challenges at the time only partially known.

Sharing Tea

Kahlil and Fatima traveled with their clans together during the first years of the tribe's trip. There was, however, a sad awareness that ultimately, they would reach the point where they would have to split. This time to be dreaded, weighed heavily on their hearts and seemed to speed the journey to the unwelcome time when one clan would set out across the edge of a great, flat expanse of dessert, while the other chose a craggy, mountain route believed the more difficult but also shorter route. The elders of the clans envisioned their journey's ends the same; abundant grazing lands and plenty of water from oasis springs, and a deep, ancient aquifer whose springs fed a great expansive lake.

Each clan exchanged a blood pledge to share, upon arrival, the land they found and that, with Allah's blessing, would sustain coming generations. It was agreed among the elders and pledged in blood as well, that when the clans were reunited, Kahlil and Fatima, and two other younger couples, would be permitted to marry as had earlier been arranged. Hassan, Kahlil's father and his clan's chieftain, said to his son that by his blood that pledge would, if necessary, someday pass to Kahlil's custody and care. It was Kahlil's solemn duty, if his father could not, to carry out the pledge when their clan reached the land near the great lake and the clans reunited.

The time had come as the caravans were prepared, and with sad, furtive glances young Fatima and Kahlil set out with their clans upon their separate journeys. Before they left, however, one afternoon as they were herding animals back to their make shift pens, the two young budding lovers agreed that no matter how long it took, Kahlil would find Fatima and they would marry. But the clans' journeys were long and arduous; seemingly unending was the long slog, to the great, expansive lake with its promise of a better life and the continuity of the clans' ancient tribal ways. More years than imagined had passed. Hassan had died in a fall and Kahlil, despite his youthful age, through blood lines, become his clan's chief. But it would take more than blood lines, and skill, insight and enormous will were required for Kahlil to wield a chieftain's influence and power within the clan. These were traits young Kahlil seemed capable of summoning at ease. Through those years, Kahlil bore, without any regret, the responsibility of honoring the pledge that was given by Fatima's clan to his father and in turn entrusted to his care.

"Kahlil lead his people, Michael, to that lake's shore", said Hamad.

"And Fatima and her clan, he found them?" asked Michael excitedly.

"No Michael, I'm sorry to say, the story goes on that he did not" replied Hamad.

Michael grimaced, his face twisted into a tortured questioning expression. He had anticipated a different outcome. This revelation was unsettling to him.

"But Michael, that is not the end of the story", implored Hamad.

Michael's head nodded slightly, several times. Only a peregrine hawk, the swiftest bird of prey in flight, would discern the otherwise imperceptible hunching shoulders. Michael's arms and hands opened, unfolding a mere few inches, but the body language translated easily—finish the story.

"You see, Michael" Hamad resumed, "as soon as Kahlil had overseen the hurried encampment of his clan near the best grazing lands they had seen in years, he set out with two members of his clan, two cousins who had also been parties to the original pledge with Fatima's clan, to find them and Fatima and reunite."

Hamad then took Michael through the story, all the way to its end. The weathered Bedouins were an intimidating sight as they rode atop the rugged camels that bore them along their often-tortured journey. Together, man and beast connected with a survivor's bond, they cast a fearsome aura passing by the suspicious eyes of villagers unaccustomed to seeing such fierce looking men. The local residents - men, women and children - turned quickly away and entered the small buildings (their homes presumably) that lined the village streets, closing the doors behind in frenzied urgency. The village was comfortable with and depended on the traveling merchant class that regularly came to barter, but these were no merchants these wild looking things that the desert had released.

One peddler, seated by a stand of mats and baskets, made no effort to retreat inside, and so Kahlil and his cousins halted, dismounted and approached the peddler. As Kahlil came closer he saw the peddler's clouded eyes and realized the peddler was blind.

"I can't see, but I can smell you and I heard the village doors closing, so I know you are not among the merchants that stop by our village as they ply their wares across the trade routes. They stop here and rest for several days, before heading west and then making the great turn on a long trek south. Are you in need of mats or baskets, friends, what do you have to exchange" asked the peddler.

"Please be at ease, I have no enemies, anyone, especially strangers are welcome to stop at my stand. I thrive on lively conversation. My dear wife

Sharing Tea

will prepare *shay* to share if you can stay awhile and tell me what brings you here today."

"I am Kahlil, these are my cousins, Hakim and Ali, we have traveled for many years to find the lake outside your village, and we seek another clan that broke off on a different route to come to this place," his voice clearly conveying the significance of his search.

Abdul was the peddler's name, his wife was A'isha, and they were gracious hosts to Kahlil and his cousins. The *shay* did not disappoint and in the conversation, Kahlil learned much about the village and that it served mostly as a stopping point, not a destination. This distinction was not unnoticed by Kahlil and his clan when they arrived. True the grazing land was lusher than any they had seen along the way, but the lake was not as large and did not expand across the great distance rumor had alleged. When the *shay* was finished, Kahlil again asked if the peddler had news of Fatima's clan.

The peddler answered that he could not be certain but a year ago, perhaps two, a clan like Kahlil's he thought, had come on a hard journey only to be disappointed that the lake was not as large as they had expected. The clan stayed for a month outside the village in the grazing lands before heading west skirting the desert and then turning south for a long trek to another great lake that legend claims sends smoke that thunders in the sky. "Mosi-O-Tunya, I have been told, is what it's called," said Abdul.

The news was disquieting to the cousins. Kahlil felt his soul quiver but fought with Herculean effort to keep his damaged psyche suppressed. They returned to the clan's camp. It was a somber, silent ride back. That evening Kahlil called a clan meeting. He asked Ali and Hakim to deliver the news of the fate of Fatima's clan, so the elders had an opportunity to digest the circumstances. Most within the clan, after all the journey had taken more years than anticipated, had already speculated there would be no reunion. Kahlil, as chief, would make the final decision and he had made up his mind what the clan must do, but the males of the clan were to be respected and as chief he must give them the opportunity to converse and offer their advice. They would advise, he would listen, he would decide; that was the way of the clan.

The clan was torn between several primary options. A few, the weariest and those who death had touched their families on the disappointing trek suggested it was time to give up the restless life and settle in the village. Some agreed, to one extent, and argued for abandoning any thought of a further journey to reunite with Fatima's clan. These men were plainly skeptical of the promise of another great lake, Mosi-O-Tunya or whatever its name might be. The journey had been difficult and a few of these men were aged, empty shells of the self that embarked on this search. Stay, but do not turn away entirely from the clan way and become a village dweller. Make permanent settlement, they proposed, where their herds now grazed by the lake that disappointed. Others argued that the journey must continue, there was a pledge between the clans to find the other and reunite; besides young men and women had arrangements made and time was running short if those bartered unions were to bear fruit. The clan needed more children, and soon. Otherwise, the next generation would not be sufficient to sustain the clan and its way of life.

When the men were tired of debating and the conversations no longer waxed and waned, Kahlil knew it was time to end the mental anguish and torture that ripped at the clan's collective soul. He quietly, as calmly as a hardened chieftain could muster, said there was another way. He called it a middle path. He said, with unshakeable determination, they were a nomadic people. It was unthinkable that they would ever be village dwellers. But no more unthinkable than resuming what Kahlil now saw as a fool's errant misstep. He would not take his people into greater peril. They would not follow Fatima's clan. The search to find some place once imagined that would free the clan from its hard way of life, and ease the heavy burden of pain and suffering, must end. "The fate of Fatima's clan rests with Allah, not our clan," proclaimed Kahlil.

He said, "I have a middle path that saves our soul, yet allows our bodies to recover and restore. We will stay here outside the village and tend our herds this season. We will barter, when we can, with the village and traveling merchant caravans. And when the seasons cycle, we will take up our tents and move to another grazing area that skirts the land along the shores of what we now call the *Lake that Disappoints*. We will not, in full measure, abandon our ancestors' way of life. The way of the clan will survive, and with Allah's blessing may we once again thrive."

The next morning Kahlil had a parchment scroll inscribed that told of the long journey of his clan to *The Lake that Disappoints*. The scroll left the fate of Fatima and her clan unanswered. Kahlil kept that scroll on his person for many years. Then one day, when he had aged to the point that he needed a staff to walk any considerable distance, he summoned his young grandson.

Sharing Tea

"Ishmael go into my tent and ask your grandmother for a sack, an empty jar, a goat skin sheath, a loaf of bread and some figs. You and I, and the younger camel, are going on a two-day journey south. We will stop first at the lake for water. Now, be quick, I have no time to waste."

Centuries later, a team of archeologists were exploring small caves in a modest range of craggy mountains to the south of a large dry lake bed. The mountains were the gatekeepers to the great desert that sprawled out southward nearly a thousand miles. In one of those caves they discovered a single earthen jar that contained a parchment scroll wrapped inside a woven sack. When scholars had the opportunity to further examine the scroll in a university laboratory, they observed a smudged area on the end of the scroll. They had no explanation for the smudge other than concluding the damage existed at the time the scroll was placed in the jar. Later, when the scroll was finally translated, the story of Kahlil's and Fatima's tribe and their clans' journeys came to light and became folklore of the people whose ancestors traced linage back to these nomadic tribes.

"The scholars never explained the smudge," inquired Michael.

"That's right," Hamad replied. "The romantics say that the smudge came from Kahlil's tears, tears of uncontained joy he had hoped to experience when Fatima and the remnants of her clan returned to the *Lake that Disappointed,* after abandoning, barely a year later, the harsh search for Mosi-O-Tunya." Hamad paused a moment before he continued.

"I'm told other accounts have been given," he said to Michael, "but it is my grandfather's that seems to me the most likely. Grandfather said the scroll was never written in the belief that Kahlil and Fatima would ever meet again. Once he heard the peddler's story Kahlil knew he would never again seek out his Fatima, he would never see her again. The smudges were caused by Kahlil's tears, but only in recognition that the moment for reunion had vanished, blow to dust by the desert's winds."

Nineteen years had passed. Michael never learned of Hamad's fate, had he and his family survived Muammar Gaddafi's coup ousting the ruling family's King Idris in 1969, and putting himself in power as Chairman of the Revolutionary Command Council. Wheelus Air Base was closed not long after when Gaddafi revoked the lease and demanded U.S. troops leave. Michael never learned of Ajax's fate or the other sentry dogs assigned to that base. He hoped they had a chance to serve on other military stations but thought that was likely not the case. Michael did not marry Mary Beth, she could not wait for him to return to Michigan and married a local man who had a deferment from the draft.

Michael left the Canine Corp, he followed a previously decided intent to volunteer for a special forces post, a para-rescue unit within the Air Force that went in warm's way to rescue downed pilots during the Vietnam War. It was, in part, his escape route from the pain he saw as a betrayal of love; a betrayal he did not want to soon face. But the decision was not the exclusive result of a desire to withdraw as he also felt a sense of duty, deep within his psyche, to do all in his power to help with rescues—he called them mercy missions among his fellow blue-bereted air force equivalent of special forces. He believed to his core that downed airmen deserved no less, and it was Michael's honor to bring them safely out of danger, and in some cases, where the outcome was unfavorable to retrieve the bodies of comrades lost to war. In a secret mission that crossed the border into Cambodia, he was gravely wounded while helping extract a downed pilot and his navigator who had escaped the crash of their F-15. He, in turn, was airlifted to a U.S. military hospital, and that is where he met Captain Aiko Hana Johnson, a Japanese American, U.S. Army surgeon, who was the military physician who extracted a bullet from his lung and saved his life. His lung had long since healed but another bullet that shattered his right shoulder left the arm impaired.

Smoke rose from the searing steaks that Michael was grilling. His back was turned to the French doors that lead back into the house from the grill that was built into the stone wall, a mere three feet high, that rimmed their outdoor patio. The wall had a smooth tile top ideal for sitting. The view down toward San Francisco Bay and the ocean was breath taking and beautiful. When the fog drifted in from the Pacific, it reminded Michael of the Mediterranean Sea and coastal Libya.

Aiko looked out and worried that her husband had lost focus on the steaks.

"Bobby, Bobby," she called out. "Please watch, don't burn the filets, you know the kids and I like ours close to rare."

"Brandon," Aiko said. "Go check on your father and rescue our beef before it is as tough as jerky."

"Dad, dad, I think the steaks are done," Brandon called out.

His teenage son's imploring voice brought him back from memories of Ramadan and Hamad and the smell of camel cooking and smoking on the spit. Bobby, he was Bobby to his wife and closest friends, used the meat fork in his left hand to place the steaks on a plate and then turned with a smile toward his son. Brandon saw the hat his father wore with pride. The ball cap was embossed with a Silver Star, emblematic of the country's third highest decoration for valor in combat. Brandon stared for a moment and noticed his father's eyes were filled with water.

Recognizing his young son's concern, Michael said, "It's the smoke son, nothing else."

But Brandon persisted, "it's that damned war, isn't it dad? It haunts you. So many protested, and no one understood your sacrifice."

"It was my duty Brandon, my moral obligation."

"It has taken me a long time to realize this truth, Brandon, and it has been a personal trail of tears along the way but my sacrifice," Michael continued, "was no greater, no less, than those who believed it their moral responsibility to protest the war, to not stand by in silence to something they believed to be morally wrong, to resist the draft often in face of great personal consequences because they believed the war was unjust, and for others, true conscientious objectors who simply could not conscientiously be party to the death of another human being. These people, I slowly came to realize were never my enemies."

"I am at peace, Brandon, with that damned war. Finally, I can accept the fact that we were just part of different armies called to action in face of a crisis in conscience. Neither stood aside in silence and cowardly inaction."

"Now, that is different Brandon," Michael said empathically, his face growing red in anger, "from those who dodged the draft but still supported the war."

"I detest those people who were gung-ho for sending American troops into harm's way, if someone other than themselves or members of their families would not have to sacrifice their bodies, their lives, and sometimes their souls to the cruel realities of war and the slaughter left in its harsh wake. They were cheerleaders for war, who hid like cowards from a moral choice, and escaped the ravages and inhumanity that happens during wars, or took on the difficult mantle of peaceful protest and civil disobedience. Those people, the war criers who did not fight, were the cowards, not the protesters, and not the soldiers who may have fought with reservations and with doubt. And there should to be a special place in hell reserved just for them—the war criers," Michael said to his son.

Michael paused, and Brandon barely heard him sigh before he said, "But that was so long ago."

"And besides," Michael said with a playful grin, "if hadn't been for that damned war, I never would have met your mother, and..." And then, he stood silent, noticing his son's slight blush.

"Brandon, take the steaks into Mom," said Michael.

"I'll be there in a second. Oh, and please tell your Mom that tonight on the patio after dark, we will dispense with our traditional Japanese tea ceremony. Tonight, I will be brewing *shay* for us to sip and enjoy."

James McCollum, US Air Force, Military Police, K-9 Corps,
Sentry Dog Ajax, Wheelus A.F.B, Tripoli, Libya March-April 1967

Philosophy

An Essay on the Question of God: A Travel Journey, the Odyssey of My Mind

PROLOGUE

FROM MY EARLY CHILDHOOD, the question of God has perplexed my mind and tormented my soul. Now, months before I turn 70, I finally feel a sense of urgency to put on paper the question that has excited and inflamed, motivated and inspired, and agonized my mind and tortured my soul for nearly 60 years. I have no health crisis, or some unwelcome dread. What compels me now is just the simple registry that time is meted out in finite measures of opportunity, a chain of circumstances that lapse for those who lose sight of life's unrelenting pulse.

The dawning of this emergent sense of urgency began as my wife Donna and I were packing for a nine-day cruise on Royal Caribbean's *Navigator of the Seas* out of Miami to three islands of the Netherland "Dutch" Antilles—the ABC's; Aruba, Bonaire and Curacao. We have cruised many times before, and will again, but never have I devoted the time I did on that cruise to gazing at the ocean and the sky and rising in the morning or setting out at night, and in moments of semi-conscious inspiration feverishly scribing thoughts in the writing journal that I brought along for that precise purpose.

My mind has wrestled with the *God Question* and traveled a twisted path since the early advent of reason's prodding awareness. Like a bird, my journey has been a migratory flight from one perilous perch to another;

never roosting long, never comfortable and secure, always moving in a recurring search for something more.

I was baptized a Roman Catholic. My mother, of Croatan and Slavic heritage, was a Catholic. My father, whose family came to America as exiles from a failed rebellion in Scotland in the 1600s and were the first family to settle in Austintown, Ohio, was raised a Baptist, but never practiced religion, in my memory, until later in his life when he converted to my mother's Catholic faith. As a young boy, aged 10 or so, I thought I had a religious calling. I would be a Catholic priest someday. God was stirring, my soul was on fire. What greater purpose could a 10-year-old envision than service to the almighty, all-powerful, Supreme Being who always was and always will be—the God of all creation.

I found something rooted, somewhere deep inside my psyche, that looked with hope and solace to a cloistered life prescribed by ritual and withdrawal from life's ordinary plight. I loved the Latin Mass and its rhythmic chants without understanding the meaning of more than a few Latin words. But intuitively, I embraced the mystery and awe the words intoned in song and, yes, too in what I later came to realize were parroted responses that left me hollow, disenchanted and unsatisfied. But at 10, I was drawn with some unexplained fascination to the Franciscans, and the brown hooded robes and sandals that branded their order.

Today, nearly 60 years later, my personal revelation is the realization that the cloistered life reflects some deep seeded primordial urge to withdraw from life, to find safety and solace inside a protected space. It is the longing, imprinted in our genetic code, to return to the womb, the safe harbor none voluntarily choose to leave. This primordial urge more, I sense, than Freud's insights into the Oedipus and Electra complexes, defines the human condition—the universal fear of aging, disintegration, death, extinguishment and nothingness. In confession, I must acknowledge 60 years was a long time to think before the moment of awareness fully awakened in my mind.

It seems that by age 12 I had the beginning awareness that I might not have a true religious calling. It happened on the boy's playground at St. Brendan's elementary school. At the time, the classrooms were not co-educational, and girls and boys were segregated from each other. We even had separate playgrounds on different sides of the church and the connected school. The girls, upon reflection, I guess to no surprise, were relegated to the church's paved parking lot. Still today, in the United States and elsewhere across the globe women struggle for equality and equal rights. In some cultures, and under some regimes, women suffer from male domination in total subjugation and humiliating soul-chilling oppression. Our collective soul is tarnished by women's plight and what each of us should shout out in an angry, anguished cry, "this is a violation of basic human rights."

But back to St. Brendan's parking lots, and the boy's recess area, that in addition to a parking lot included a grass playing field, to lay out the unraveling of my religious call. I place the blame on the native puberty that comes with all its clumsy hormonal changes wreaking havoc in its path to unsuspecting girls and boys. A few boys had gathered to check out a book with photos of scantily clad women that one boy had smuggled to school that day. But our attempt to slyly turn the pages was interrupted by the rapid approach of our fifth-grade teacher Mr. Caparossi. Our attempts at stealth were not as surreptitious as we expected, and in horror (feigned for effect, or real, I do not know today) Mr. Caparossi wrenched the book from the terrified boy's hands. Moments later he pulled me aside (I was, at least before that incident, a favored pupil) and asked imploringly "don't you still want to be a priest?" I shrugged my shoulders and meekly said, "I'm not sure, I might also want to be a lawyer." How ironic, the words were a prophecy. My religious call seemingly expired that day on St. Brendan's playground. Years later, I studied the law, earned a juris doctor degree, scored in the top two-percent on the national multi-state bar examination, was admitted to the Ohio bar and licensed to practice law, received an appointment as a state assistant attorney general, and served as university counsel at a mid-sized, public university in Youngstown, Ohio, nestled in the Mahoning and Shennago Valley that stretches almost imperceptibly, other than for the price of tuition, into Pennsylvania past the city of Sharon and farther on to New Castle.

By age 14 or 15 I was afflicted with a growing doubt. The Question of God had begun to intrude into my consciousness. The germ had infiltrated my mind and I could not find an antibiotic that would stop its spread. I rejected, in quiet misery, not only my Catholic religious education, but all of Christianity, and even more, I began to doubt the existence of God at all. I was tortured. I could not reconcile the inconsistency in believing there was some supreme being that was all-holy, all-knowing, all-powerful, all-just, and all-merciful; yet allowed hunger and abject poverty to exist alongside opulent wealth. How, I asked myself, could a compassionate God who was supposed to love the creatures and majesty of its creation allow hatred, oppression, cruelty and barbarism to flourish? How can this possibly be; had God abandoned us? Or, did he even exist? To my young searching mind these glaring inconsistencies tore at my heart and challenged my soul to its core. I could discern only one meaning; that God, if he did exist had absconded and abandoned man. God was dead, I was beginning to conclude, and I was about to bury him and any hope that I once had for personal salvation. Nothing was immortal, not God, not the earth, not the universe, and most of all not me.

Into adulthood I came. I was restless. I was cursed with a mind that seemed to understand and grudgingly accept, that salvation—a personal, permanent self—was a fundamental coping mechanism encoded in our primitive ancestor's brains, a mythological underpinning that assuaged and managed the potentially unruly spirit of the masses. If there was so much misery, injustice, pain and suffering, with dreaded death its ultimate end, then surely humanity had every reason to hope, to believe that life was only a temporary mode. How else could men cope? God in heaven, or wherever it resided, was permanent and connected to our souls, and our spirits traveled on beyond this earthly place. We exist, we persist, death is a portal not an end, this belief was the fuel that birthed religion and painted a thousand faces for God and his creation. But I resisted and rejected this dream of an immortal, eternal, enduring self. I saw, at that time, only the cold and darkness that stands at the edge of the abyss. There absolute stillness reigns and nothingness obtains. It looms for all of us: the good, the bad, the heroic, the cowardly, the compassionate, the indifferent, the loving and the cruel. We all face the same fate.

There I languished and anguished for several years until I discovered the writings of Nikos Kazantzakis, and later still the teachings of the Buddha. I have drawn upon their writings, and both have been my teachers and beloved companions. To them my mind has gravitated. I am now, for lack of better description, a relentless questioner. But I no longer despair. I embrace the value of all life. Life in all forms, however short, is sacred. Near a point of exhaustion, my troubled mind has, at least temporarily put aside its endless searching, and found an evasive peace. I embrace the truth that living this life as best as we are able is purpose enough. Life is its own purpose and needs no other validation.

PREPARATIONS

Shortly before we began packing for our cruise to the Netherlands "Dutch" Antilles, I saw an internet post that served as an additional motivation to begin writing. In that post, Pope Francis had acknowledged that a belief in God did not negate the scientific evidence supporting the Big Bang theory of creation of the universe nor the evolution of species on planet earth. Francis said the science behind both theories was strong, and that God was not some magician that waves a magic wand. I found it refreshing that the leader of the Roman Catholic church did not support the notion that God was related to the wizards in one of J. K. Rowling's Harry Potter books. This pope has made other pronouncements that have warmed my heart toward his awareness of humanity's suffering and the need for compassion and charity.

Born Jorge Mario Bergoglio, in Buenos Aires, Argentina, on December 17, 1936, a member of the Order of the Society of Jesus. Francis is the first Jesuit pope, and the first pope from the Americas (South or North), and the first non-European pope since the eighth century. He chose the papal name of Francis, in honor of Saint Francis of Assisi, the founder of the Franciscan Order and an adopted patron of animals and the environment. It is no accident, I believe, that Pope Francis is such a strong spokesperson against the reckless exploitation of our planet. He attributes the rape of planet earth to unbridled greed, avarice, and the quest for and accumulation of wealth in the hands of fewer and fewer people in the world. His decision to live in more modest quarters of the Vatican hotel, rather than the more opulent Papal apartment in the Vatican's Apostolic Palace is a symbolic attempt to mirror his actions to his words.

To be clear, in my opinion Pope Francis is no Dali Lama or Buddha, he accepts most traditional Catholic doctrine on the ordination of priests, the role of women in the church, priestly celibacy and sexual orientation. He, like the church itself has been slow to confront child sexual abuse within the church. (I should note that the Catholic church has no monopoly on the sexual abuse of children. There are other Christian denominations and religions that are equally complicit with clerical abuse of children, young girls and boys). It is Francis' humility and openness not to condemn good people who do not fit neatly into long accepted and expected roles, that sets him apart from his predecessors. No one, including this Pope, can change overnight an ancient institution entrenched for centuries in its dogma and beliefs. But as a major religious leader, his words matter. When he speaks out calling for compassion toward the horrendous plight of immigrants, while the American president would ban all Muslim immigrants and build a wall across the entire southern border of the United States to keep out Mexicans and other Central American refugees and rip young children from their parent's arms and cruelly separate families fleeing certain terror and probable death, Francis is the voice of human pity for the misfortune of those trapped in untenable places. When Francis said, who am I to judge gays, his was a voice against the marginalization of so many good, loving people, who historically have been vilified, and remain victims of discrimination and hatred. And he is a contemporary prophet whose words persistently condemn the new cult of money and the economic and social dictatorship that the golden calf-cult worships.[1]

TRAVELOGUE

I had my suitcases for the Netherlands Antilles cruise packed ten days in advance. Other than writing, it appears I have an obsessive compulsion to not wait until I am rushed to complete a task. This gave me time to begin my travel journal ahead of the cruise.

2/15/2017

I find it rather ironic that the authors of the Book of Genesis (whose origins are tied to ancient nomadic tribes), with no scientific expertise, inadvertently articulated what I find as the most profound intuitive insight into reality inscribed in the Old Testament. My paraphrase—"In the beginning there was darkness, and then there was light, and God created the heavens and the earth."There it is, if you only open your eyes and your ears—an insightful articulation of the explosive creation of the universe and its evolution ("the heavens"), and the evolution of our planet ("the earth") and its lifeforms, including all its plants and animals, and oh, yes, humans too.

For eons, beginning in caves with our most primitive human ancestors, we have been trying to paint images that give substance to the being(s) or force(s) that created us and the world we inhabit. From cave drawings depicting the life sustaining hunts of early man, to shamans communing with a spirit world beyond this earthly existence, to priestly castes and their closely guarded rites holding sway and demanding faithful loyalty to religious rituals, practice and beliefs, man has tried desperately to find a face that defines the mystery and awe we call God. The puzzle and the quest remain. It is this unresolved conundrum that bedevils my mind and for 60 years tormented my soul. I fully acknowledge that despite my embrace of the explosive Big Bang theory and the subsequent unfolding evolution of the universe, there remains the nagging, unsettling conundrum of how, where, when and what caused this to happen.

For an answer, I have come to rely on a term that scientists have labeled for other purposes as the *God Particle*. Thus, before any beginning there is infinity—total darkness and an expanse of cold across all time and space. In this apparent nothingness, the *God Particle* existed; it always did. All the mass and energy that ever was, is, and will be was compressed and contained in the *God Particle* - into this point of singularity, this origin of the past, keeper of the chaotic present, and harbinger of an endless unduplicated future. The *God Particle* compressed and confined, until the innate pressure to fill the void of nothingness—infinity—could no longer be contained. The *God Particle* exploded in a burst of light and boiling energy, hurling matter (all the matter that makes up our universe) outward from the point of singularity. This creative surge is the birth giver of everything since; trillions and trillions of stars, billions of galaxies, planets, species (plants, animals, alien life for sure)—all evolving from that point, all living, disintegrating, dying and being refashioned, reborn. And the *God Particle* is the essence within everything—you and I, our nurturing and destructive planet, our galaxy, the billions of other galaxies, and trillions of stars that are our universe. We are one with the *God Particle*, all evolving, all alive, all disintegrating, all dying, all being repurposed, all being reborn; forever a part of our creator—the *God Particle*.

As a caveat, my reliance on the *God Particle* is one of imagery, and has no direct scientific connection with the theory, first postulated in the 1960s, of the Higgs Boson and particle physics. That theory is the object of an intense international research project involving thousands of scientists and engineers from around the globe who collaborated on the underground construction of the Large Hadron Collider near Geneva, Switzerland. An international research team uses the collider to test various theories of particle physics, as well as trying to measure the theoretical properties of the Higgs Boson and our understanding of the origin of the mass of subatomic particles. But to make my point again, I chose the imagery of the *God Particle* to provide a visual context for the creative force of the universe, not just for my readers, but for my own edification as well.

Now it was a time to pause, put down my pen, close my journal, reflect some more, and explore if and how the *God Particle* resembles the human heart as it beats and expands and contracts.

2/16/2017

Inspiration or insight often comes to me in that state of semiconscious sleep, when I am aware of my brain's rumination, but lie not totally awake. It comes mostly in night's sleep but also during naps, sometimes before sleep begins and the onslaught of unconscious dreams unfold and sometimes just before emerging from the deeper slumber of unconsciousness.

Today, I decided to put aside writing for a week or more and do some further background reading to prepare for the writing I was planning to do on the cruise, and after perhaps a 10-year gap, I carefully reread in its entirety (for the sixth or so time in my life) Nikos Kazantzakis' The Saviors of God: Spiritual Exercises.

Although I put aside further exposition of the *God Particle*, I did not totally abandon writing during the interlude that ensued for my background preparation. But I could not shut down entirely the creative urge that I had just released. So, yes, I did record an occasional isolated thought that surfaced, either spontaneously on their own from some earlier observation, or that was spurred by something that resonated within one of the books I was then reviewing. And so, in total randomness, I jotted notes down in the travel journal that I would later use to better shape my writing during our cruise to the Netherlands "Dutch" Antilles.

For years, I was growing increasingly frustrated with the faux ideology of many evangelical, Christian fundamentalists. As an example, I was sickened by the vile hatred and bigotry that the fringe Westboro Baptist Church spewed toward members of the LGBTQ community and a woman's right to control her own body and chose what was best for her. Their rhetoric and

An Essay on the Question of God

actions were, and are, the antithesis of Christ's teachings of love, acceptance and compassion. So, I recorded Amos 5:21–24 from the Old Testament where Jehovah according to the scribe who recorded Amos' words is purported to say:

> *I hate, I despise your festivals,*
> *and take no delight in your solemn assemblies.*
> *Even though you offer me your . . . offerings . . .*
> *I will not accept them . . . I will not look upon them.*
> *Take away the noise of your songs; I will not listen . . . .*
> *But let justice roll down like waters*
> *and righteousness like an ever-flowing stream.*

My profound consternation with the American political landscape and the election of a person often characterized by pundits as a charlatan, misogynist, fascist leaning, demagogue as President of the United States, puts me in a state of dread and despair. These opinions, based upon a compelling body of reported evidence, are difficult to explain away. Investigations may ultimately provide evidence that the 2016 presidential election was tainted and the product of a series of collusions with a foreign government (Russia) that preferred the election of an Orwellian figure as more favorable to Russian interests. Meanwhile, I cannot, and have not, withheld my public commentary on how unfit, how corrupt, how immoral, how consumed with greed and the accumulation of wealth, how devoid of compassion and human empathy for those less fortunate and struggling, and how oblivious to the rape of the planet that sustains all earthly life, is this person, perhaps unequaled in a narcissist personality, who controls the mightiest military force and nuclear arsenal on the planet. In this troubled time, I have scribed in my journal as a constant reminder of John F. Kennedy's loosely drawn inspiration, as well as Martin Luther King, Jr's adaptation from Dante Alighieri's *The Inferno, canto iii*, with Dr. King's adaptation adding the second sentence as follows: "The darkest places in hell are reserved for those who maintain their neutrality in times of moral crisis. There comes a time when silence becomes betrayal." The actual language in Wadsworth's translation of *The Inferno, canto iii* casts the silent, like those who stood silent during the Nazi holocaust or more recently the Charlotte white supremacy march, as outcasts despised by God and the Devil equally, and ostracized by both from heaven and hell alike. Wadsworth's 1867 translation follows:

> *And he to me: This miserable mode*

> *Maintain the melancholy souls of those*
> *Who lived withouten infamy or praise.*
> *Comingled are they with that caitiff choir*
> *Of Angels, who have not rebellious been,*
> *Nor faithful were to God, but were to self.*
> *The heavens expelled them, not to be less fair:*
> *Nor them the nevermore abyss receives ...* [2]

The last note I included before leaving on the cruise was from Kazantzakis' The Saviors of God. It is here that Kazantzakis set our individual responsibility to act, to save the world as if we are its last, its only hope for survival and salvation, and if we fail then all is lost. This, I believe, is the spiritual force that drives all *Great Souls*—the compelling awakening that all are saved, or none are saved! We are a collective soul, connected inseparably with all of nature, all of creation.

As I finished transcribing these thoughts, I reflected to that time in adolescence when skepticism had disturbed my comfort with religion. More broadly, doubt was preparing to enter my psyche and ultimately alter my nascent discomfort with the very idea of God. What had intruded, and I began to obsess about, was the irrefutable, irreconcilable difference (the great conundrum) contrasting an all-powerful supreme being and all-merciful compassionate creator. The Christian, in my case Catholic, concept of hell could not exist if the creator was a merciful God. I could not accept as real, a place of eternal horror. No merciful creator could ever relegate the creatures of his creation to such a vile place for all eternity. The mental images in Dante's story of his journey through hell in the *Divine Comedy's Inferno*, and the visual images of Botticelli's *Map of Hell* and a host of other artists including Bosch and Dali might strike fear into the faithful and believers but left me shivering and empty; no fear was strong enough to overcome my revulsion and rejection of this perverse perspective. Equally incredulous was the Christian belief in heaven itself. What noble, heroic, erect human, I asked myself, wants to spend an eternity singing songs of praise and bowing obsequiously, like a servile slave, to some giant narcissistic supreme being? This seemed, to me, more like hell than some form of reward in eternal bliss. Surely, if paradise existed then Christians have this one dead wrong.

This was my silent suffering and at the time I had no allies with a common cause. I felt, if I had spoken out, I would have been chastised as an arrogant adolescent, or a rebellious teenager trying to assert my independence from convention. Also, at the time I suffered from intellectually insecurity. I lacked self-confidence and felt intellectually inferior to classmates who earned good grades. It wasn't until I graduated from high school, was in the military, and to salvage my personal identity turned to reading as a path to salvation, that I grew confident in my own intellectual prowess. The insecurity largely disappeared, but even now as I write with the intent to publish, the residual dust of that insecurity tugs at my mind; will anyone, I ask myself, find cause to read what I have written.

Much later in my life I came to appreciate what was transpiring and the intellectual metamorphous that I was undergoing. This was the slowly emerging maturation of my own vision, my peculiar window into eternity. It was a process that I could not rush. It had to evolve on its own, I could not simply will my enlightenment. Experience, insight and finally intuition had to ignite my awakening. What I was beginning to intuit, as a young man emerging out of adolescence, was the unfolding awareness that humans, from our earliest ancestor's painting the hunting ritual on the walls of caves, have been searching for a spirit world. Lead by shamans, and later the priestly caste, humans have desperately been in search for a haven. We have pursued the creator that has afflicted our existence with nature's depredations from the time our species split from our simian cousins.

We humans have yearned for some escape from the suffering and fear that is the driving force of life; the suffering attendant to aging and decay, and the fear of death and foreshadowing of non-existence. Heaven, and its spiritual plane where the individual - the self - endured, was the soothing aloe that assuaged the compelling need to believe mortal life was only a portal to something free of chaos and decay. But I could not gravitate to an eternity of imposed adulation. Now, in my awakened condition, I understand that instinctively, the human quest is one of freedom; to be free of pain and suffering. My mind is clear on this: freedom is not heaven; freedom is not a place or ultimate destination; freedom is a state of mind!

3/2/2017; Miami

Donna and I flew from Philadelphia non-stop to Miami on March 2, 2017, a day ahead of embarkation on the *Navigator of the Seas.* We stayed at a hotel in downtown Miami only several miles from the Port of Miami. That was Thursday and we walked a block and a half to our dinner reservation at Perricone's Marketplace and Café. We arrived with umbrellas in hand

Philosophy

barely a minute ahead of a heavy rain. We had tasty Italian dishes, Donna had two lemon-drop martinis (her favorite) and I enjoyed two glasses of sauvignon blanc, a switch for me from the usual merlot or cabernet reds. The rain cascaded off the transparent plastic roof that covered what once must have been an outdoor patio section of the restaurant. We were in no hurry, and slowly sipped our second drinks waiting for the rain to subside and hopefully stop. In South Florida rain often comes and goes quickly, and that was the case as we did not need our umbrellas for the walk back to the hotel. Donna and I both were impressed with how vibrant and safe downtown Miami appeared to us. This is a city trying hard to be a destination for entrepreneurs and the millennials that are drawn to jobs and the lifestyles that Miami was working hard to promote. We were not naïve to Miami's, or any other large urban city's inherent issues, but we were none-the-less impressed. After all, isn't all life a work in progress?

Earlier that day, the cab ride from Miami airport to our hotel was surprisingly informative. Our driver, we learned in conversation after sharing details of our upcoming cruise, explained that although he had lived in Miami for thirty-seven years, he was born in Haiti. Labadee, a small peninsula area isolated from the mainland, was Royal Caribbean Cruise Line's isolated beach resort at our first port call of Haiti. The cabbie, who indicated he had family in Haiti, related details about his homeland we were generally aware of from news accounts. Haiti's proclivity for natural disasters are well documented and known; earth quakes, hurricanes, torrential rains and mountain mud slides bedeviled, decimated, and impoverished this poor Caribbean island. Labadee was an aberration; the telltale signs of poverty and devastation carefully obscured from the cruisers who took excursions to the idyllic beaches of Labadee. But the cabbie's story of political corruption, and its toll on the island was something we had heard of, but not in the detail we heard from our loquacious driver. He described a country, crushed by the effects of rampant political corruption. He lamented that tens of millions of dollars intended for infrastructure improvements were always diverted to politicians at every level of the government, and the repairs that the donated money was designed to pay for never came to fruition. Haiti was betrayed by its own leaders, and the people's suffering continues unabated. Donna and I felt a twinge of discomfort thinking about Haiti's plight juxtaposed with our coming day of leisure on one of Ladadee's relaxing beaches. Still, we would take the planned excursion, and we had a wonderful time, temporarily blocking out the misery and corruption that existed on the mainland.

3/3/2017; Port of Miami

Our shuttle from the hotel arrived early at the Port of Miami. After processing, having our photos taken, and receiving our Sea Pass (the card used for everything on the ship, for purchases and charges, as well as entry to your stateroom), we had to wait approximately forty-five minutes to board. The *Navigator of the Seas* is part of Royal Caribbean's Voyager Class fleet. The ship has fifteen decks, weighs more than 137,300 gross tons, is 1,020 feet long, has a top cruising speed of twenty-two knots (25 miles per hour), and can accommodate over 3,114 passengers and nearly 1,200 crew members. At one time, it was the twelfth largest passenger ship on the seas. Beautiful, immense, I still marvel at the science that keeps these behemoth ships floating, many are longer than the Empire State Building is tall. We set about unpacking our luggage, changing into dinner clothes and headed to the dining room with neighbors who were wintering in Florida and drove to the Port to join us on the cruise. But just before leaving our stateroom I set out my journal, a pen, a dictionary and thesaurus, and several books I brought along for general background. Soon I would set about the task of writing, and would resume my rumination on the *God Particle,* with a hope that the aura of the ocean and the night sky would provide all the inspiration I would need to be productive.

3/3/2017 to 3/12/2017; cruising and writing

I sat in a chair on our stateroom balcony for an hour, Friday evening after dinner. I always find the ocean's motion, the sight of small white caps topping off the rolling waves, the salty moisture of the air, and the generally cloudless sky calming and inspirational. There is, to me, something mystical, something alluring, something that calls me back to a prehistoric, primordial time. "Tomorrow I start," I said silently to myself, and then again barely audible to the ocean. I wasn't sure if the ocean was listening, or if it could, but just in case I did not want to slight my traveling companion, who I trusted to help inspire my writing. We would be at sea for the first two days' journey. Saturday morning, with a cup of coffee in hand, seated on a chair on the balcony would be a perfect time to pick up with the *God Particle,* especially if I was fortunate to slowly awake to that semi-conscious state where, intuition and intellect merged. There, in that cauldron of creative inspiration, I often found that ideas coalesced into coherent concepts, sometimes providing the very sentences that flowed, from the ink in the pen I held in my hand, unto the awaiting paper—it was a birthing process, a creative surge that even today confounds and mystifies me.

3/4/2017

Dawn's early light had hardly peaked above the ocean's horizon, as I sat gazing from the balcony. It was time to revisit the *God Particle*. As I have already indicated, I have wrestled with the conundrum of creation, of impermanence, of nothingness—always searching for a synthesis, some coherent solution solving the puzzle. I reasoned, if what I see, hear, smell, touch, taste and think is no more than an illusion; still it exists, I exist if not in my own sensate awareness or dreams, then in someone else's awareness, dreams or illusions.

The first premise of the *God Particle* is the awareness, an intuitive enlightened acknowledgement, that there can be no "nothingness." Pre-existence of something is a predicate necessity of reality, infinity is not a vast, cold, dark void of nothingness. This begs the question, the great conundrum; if something is (you and I for example), then what is or are the origins of that something (of us)? It is relentless, this search, and I always circle back the question of what is or how did this something come into being. The only plausible explanation that I have been able to construct and accept is that this something always existed, and by inferred necessity must always exist. That something, I have concluded, is the *God Particle*. Now a quick note of explanation is appropriate. To give a face and substance to my emergent concept imbedded in the *God Particle* term, I rely on and use for illustration some scientific terms rooted in astronomy and physics. Much of the science of these terms lay outside my intellectual comfort zone, but the terms serve as metaphors and analogies, enabling me to create images and impressions that provide an outline and shape the contours of the concepts that I seek to expose in my writing. They are not scientific or mathematical proofs and are not intended to prove what I postulate. I have borrowed them to give the reader, and myself frankly, a glimpse, an insight into my intuitions, and the visions they invite and inform.

Although some primitive religions envisioned and depicted their gods in terrifying personas, voracious appetites, and bi-polar personalities, many other religions, and most certainly Christianity, view God through a less fear-inducing anthropomorphous lens. Archeological evidence and sacred texts provide support for this view. The bible says that God created man in his own image. A more likely scenario is that humans, although not universally, often sought to depict their gods in some human resemblance, and by implication attributed human characteristics, personalities and behaviors to their gods. This is the pathology that must be eradicated if we are to penetrate the great conundrum. Regardless of the image, the basic premise remains the same. If nothingness is not our reality, then something must have always existed, and should always do so. That something, I have labeled the *God Particle*. As I have said before, the *God Particle* is you, me, the plants and animals of the earth, the stars, the galaxies, the universe itself. All things are part of and contained within the *God Particle*.

A "beating heart" analogy provided an initial refuge for my questioning mind. Imagine, before the Big Bang and measurable time (an approximate deduction) there was always, without beginning, the *God Particle* and infinity encompassing the dark void of endless space. The *God Particle* contained and compressed into a singular point all the matter that ever was, is, and will be; compressed and contained within itself until it could no longer bear the pressure and weight. Then in a gigantic burst of light and cosmic release of boiling energy, the *God Particle* burst forth in an immense creative surge, spewing itself, its particles, across the void. These particles formed into the early stars and galaxies, then later into new stars and galaxies, and later still planets, and now within the past billion years' earth's inhabitants—sea life, plants, animals, humans, you and me. We are all a product of that primordial stew of boiling, surging *God Particles*.

I found comfort within the "beating heart" analogy. Initially, modern physics and astronomy seemed to point to an expanding and contracting universe. This helps circumvent the great conundrum of what initiated the Big Bang—who or what was the ultimate creator? Here the *God Particle*, with its beating heart, expanding and contracting as blood is pushed out and drawn in, escapes the conundrum; it has always existed, it always will. It beats, and its expansion is the creative surge that gives life to the entire universe, and inevitably elsewhere in the expanding universe. This heart beats out once in tens of billions of years and stars, galaxies, planets and species are born, disintegrate, die, and are reborn (chaotically refashioned and repurposed in a new, unfolding unduplicated reality). Then, at the outer limits of gravity's sway, the *God Particle* contracts over billions of years, imploding within itself back to the point of singularity. It compresses, and containment follows, until once again, all its particles, mass and energy are reconstituted. Momentarily, the void of infinity and total darkness obtain, then the *God Particle* can no longer be restrained and bursts with the creative surge of a Big Bang. Eternally expanding and contracting, giving birth, disintegrating, dying, re-creating in an unending cycle; each creative burst unique, random, chaotic, uncharacteristic in its unfolding. Recurring but not duplicating, giving way to the majestic randomness of creation.

This is what we are; we are one with God; the *God Particle* is one with us, with all things. When our vessel perishes, as do all things including this iteration of the universe, we are reconstituted, repurposed (our God Particle that is) to other uses and that particle that was us lives on in other forms. Our particles return as the *God Particle* contracts, exploding to new life as the *God Particle's* beating heart expands again. This is as close as the universe experiences eternal recurrence.

I was done for the day, my creative surge dissipated. I was again on a perilous perch, comfort was fleeting with an awareness that not all was perfect within the beating heart. Later, in the evening, I lay out on a lounge chair on our balcony, gazing as I often did at the ocean, renewed through its rhythmic motion, and then inspiration came in that semi-conscious state of near sleep. The next several days I turned to writing poetry. I would dive deep into my own psyche and try to release powerful images of my mind's fanciful attempt, and my soul's mournful yearning, for the search for God and the acceptance of heroic impermanence.

But that night just before giving in to sleep's beckoning, I had to record the nagging discomfort I could not dismiss with the beating heart analogy. The problem lies with the science of an expanding and contracting universe. Scientifically, the theory may not withstand further discoveries; there is some observational based evidence that suggests the possibility that our universe is ever expanding, and over hundreds of billions of years will simply vanish into the nothingness of dark, cold space. But here is the problem, my small mind, despite man's wondrous evolutionary development, cannot get beyond the need for the *God Particle*. Despite this counter scientific theory, I cannot free myself of the thought that the *God Particle* is the ultimate prime number - the something that is part of everything that ever was, is, and will be, the something that always was and did not need some external creator other than its own creative surge. This, I had intuitively experienced as the self-actualizing *God Particle*.

An Essay on the Question of God

So, what are the alternatives? Here are a few this non-scientist can raise. Black holes that serve as portals to billions of other universes; each in their own endless expansions and contractions, perhaps with different laws of physics. Or, trillions upon trillions of God Particles each within their own universe, each defying nothingness, each compressed until they can no longer be contained within themselves, each bursting into gigantic individual explosions of creative energy that expand forever across the infinity of space. The truth is that I cannot reconcile this puzzle. At some deep semi-conscious recess of my awareness of self, I still cling to an intuitive grasp, however tenuous, to a belief in the *God Particle* (Kazantzakis' cry of the imperiled God within each of us) as the only tenable insight that eliminates the need for something external to itself to explain the cycle of creation, expansion, disintegration, implosion, death and rebirth through an eternal creative surge that cannot be contained in the frightful face of infinity. This is the great conundrum, the question of God!

3/5/2017

Up early again. Before breakfast I looked over notes from the first draft of a poem I started last evening, entitled *Time Keeper*. Today, we go to a beach at Labadee. Poetry must wait until this evening or tomorrow on a day at sea. Often, I let a first draft sit for a while. What percolates up after it brews for a few days is usually a more refined writing. I left that poem alone and turned my attention back to an entry I had included in the journal as background material, on February 27, 2017, days before we embarked on our *Navigator of the Seas* cruise.

In that entry, I wrote that nearly all religions share a basic set of characteristics, fundamental elements. There are myriad ways to define religion. We can debate how many characteristics are a prerequisite, but as a guidepost I see two as universal—authority and ritual. Ritual, I believe, has a wingspan broad enough to capture tradition, a term that others might readily substitute for ritual within its embrace. At any rate, I am drawn to that perspective.

Authority is the organization of a religion into a core set of beliefs; controlled, exacted and parceled out by some variant of a priestly caste. Ritual is the mechanism the priestly caste uses to conform behavior and beliefs, and to assuage and at other times promote fear. Ritual is performed in times of celebration, joy and jubilation, and likewise in times of tribulation, regret, sorrow, suffering, and profound grief; and, yes, too, in times of rising anger. As wonderful as can be celebrations and causes for unfettered joy, I sense it is not joy but fear that leaves a primordial imprint on the souls of humans. I believe F. Max Muller's translation from Pali of a metaphor from the Buddha offers a primal insight into the Buddha's philosophy. In the Muller translation the Buddha compares a shepherd directing his cows, with a staff, into a stable to the same affect that aging, and death have in driving the lives of man.[3] To the Buddha this realization is the moment of awakening and freedom. The Buddha's insight is profound in its simplicity and in its exposition of a universal truth. Religion draws upon humanity's fear of the human condition; ultimately confronting suffering in the face of inevitable disintegration (aging) and death (non-existence). For most religions, this universal concern is the path to authority, control, and the organized traditions and rituals that often define a specific religious culture.

The suffering that the Buddha implicates as humanity's grand intimidator should not be narrowly construed to suggest that the Buddha was obsessed with only the physical pain associated with injury and disease, or the anguish that torments the mentally ill. His is the broadest possible perspective of pain, and importantly includes the fear of loss of joy and the pleasures that obtain in life; of the loss of loved ones and friends; of the loss of freedom; of the loss of art in all its inspiring forms of human expression; of the loss of celebrating the good that flows from human compassion and charity; and the loss of communion with humanity, our mother earth, - with all the plants and animals it nurtures along with us - and the universe and all the suns and galaxies with which we share infinity.

In his pilgrimage, the Buddha saw the lives of ordinary people as difficult, failing to transubstantiate to higher levels of awareness and existence (unfulfilled), and shaped by fear of suffering, disintegration and death. Within the penumbra, imbedded within the woven fabric of Kazantzakis' writings you will encounter the "noble peasant." Kazantzakis saw a hard, but honorable nobility craved into the often-unrecognized struggle of transforming the ordinary commands and tasks and daily rituals of the mundanity of existence into a larger collective struggle to impart spirituality into the daily battles of life. From my readings, it is the twentieth century American poet and novelist Robert Penn Warren, who poignantly best captures the Buddha's insight that suffering drives all life, just beyond midway, in his epic tale in verse and voices *Brothers to Dragons* where Warren's Thomas Jefferson says to his nephew, Meriwether, that pain is the universal reality unavoidably consequent to consciousness.[4]

Magic was a foot, and I was nearing a time of deep introspection and creativity; I was soon to give birth to a seminal poem, *Time Keeper*. But first I wanted to record three important concepts attributed to the Buddha and detail the stunning end of Kazantzakis' The Saviors of God. Once this was done, I sensed that a creative surge, momentarily held in check, would be released and the *Time Keeper* would soon roll out like the ocean's waves.

3/6/2017; sea day

I recorded the Buddha's three pillars of existence and the explosive end of Kazantzakis' The Saviors of God in my journal.

Like Christianity, Islam, Judaism, and many other enduring religions, Buddhism has different sects—branches from the same base tree that have grown and evolved with significant variations. The Mahayana branch of Buddhism, the branch I most comfortably align with, does not accept the concept of a personal creator god who fashioned the universe through some divine deliberate design. I call that process the creative surge of the *God Particle*. To the Buddha there were three foundational pillars that together create the synergy that defines the essence of existence. The pillars are: *anicca*, impermanence; *dukkha*, suffering; and, *anatta*, essentially the absence of a permanent self or identity.[5]

The Saviors of God ends as Kazantzakis delivers the bomb which explodes all the *Spiritual Exercises* within, ending the pilgrimage with "The Silence."[6] Proud and erect man faces the abyss and rapturously sings a lyric incantation. This, I believe is a point where Kazantzakis and the Buddha merge, both are awakened, and both confront the abyss. This is the moment of sublime silence. We have come to the end of our journey, the travelers (the hajis, the pilgrims, the mystics) have arrived in their Mecca, their Jerusalem, their Nirvana. Our personal pilgrimage toward God is over. Our individual conscious ascent toward spiritual purity is about to confront the awesome silence of the void. On the edge of the abyss ascending man stares into the silence. At this point we are stripped of every illusion. We peer deeply into the eyes of annihilation. We face the final seduction of hope, a hope that personal immortality (the enduring self) is obtainable and that God exists as some predetermined, absolute end. Kazantzakis' faith in the ethical process of the *Spiritual Exercises*, like the Buddha's insight into the Eightfold Path, has become unshakable. No idea, act or movement can destroy it because it is not based upon God, nor hope, nor fear, nor eternity.

Its safety is intact, imperious to erosion, because the insight is based upon the void.

I have learned, slowly and grudgingly, from my beloved teachers that every moment is deathless. We are among the aware, the sentient beings in a universe of the unaware. Proud and erect, as sensate creatures, in consciousness we face the abyss, the silence and its unfathomable incarnation, and defiantly burst into a song that celebrates life and does not hide from the pain that comes from the awareness that only the moment exists within the construct of our own mind and the senses that inform it within that moment.

3/7/2017; Curacao

We docked in Curacao in the morning. We are taking a tour of the island later. We generally take an excursion the first time we visit a new port of call. If we visit again, we usually go on our own with a local taxi driver to a beach or other familiar destination. I was up early and wanted to write more on yesterday's continued exploration and insight into the *God Particle*, Kazantzakis, and the Buddha.

Some critics try to label the Buddha and Kazantzakis as pessimists, fatalists, or nihilists. I reject that characterization for either. The two searchers did have in common an early infatuation with asceticism that each ultimately abandoned. Later, each would find their middle path. In common, they came to understand and accept the transcendent truth of impermanence, the transitory nature of existence, and the heroic effort and commitment involved in the transubstantiation of matter into spirit—the ascent to a higher plane of existence. The Buddha's empty bowl illustrates impermanence as well as any example I have ever encountered. My own version of the empty bowl illustration follows. Imagine a powerful urge of thirst and a bowl of water. The bowl is never full; its steady state is one of emptiness. The water is only present in the precise moment it touches your lips to quench your thirst. Glance back and the bowl is empty, and it is gone forever. Glance forward and the water is not there, the bowl is empty; its becoming is only an illusion. Only in the ephemeral, impermanent moment when the water touches your lips is it real. Ever else the bowl is empty. This, I believe, Kazantzakis and the Buddha understood was true for them; and, I assert, it is true for all of us.

My initial attempts to pronounce the name of the island of Curacao were futile and humorous. I was told I was not unique in mispronouncing the name of this southern Caribbean island that sits about forty miles off the South American coast of Venezuela. The proper pronunciation sounds like *Kure-a-sow*, with the second "c" being soft like an "s."

We debarked from the ship for our island excursion at the capital city of Willemstad. Dutch and Spanish architectural styles dominate the capital city that developed along the natural harbor that obviously influenced the early development of this location. The buildings, except for government buildings which were painted white, were a free-for-all of pastels. From a distance, the buildings resembled multi-colored impressionist paintings like Vincent van Gogh's "irises" or Claude Monet's "water lilies." In a brief history lesson provided by the tour guide, as our bus moved through the capital city, we learned that the original inhabitants of Curacao are believed to be Amazon basin Indians who likely migrated around the thirteenth or fourteenth centuries. The Spanish were the first Europeans to arrive on the island around the end of fifteenth century. Then came an influx of Dutch colonists and Sephardic Jews who began to immigrate once the Dutch West India Company had founded the harbor city that would become Curacao's capital of Willemstad. The economy of the small island, with a population of around 150,000 permanent residents, depended successively upon the slave trade, salt mining, and the oil industry, until each enterprise in turn lost its economic viability. Tourism is now the main economy of Curacao and the other Netherlands Dutch Antilles islands. In 2010 Curacao became one of three Dutch Antilles islands with the independent status of a country within the Kingdom of the Netherlands, with its own parliament, prime minister and judiciary but with the Netherlands retaining responsibility for foreign affairs and defense.

As we traveled out of the city we rode past several churches, mainly roman catholic (the predominant religion on the island), nearly all connected with a nearby elementary school and often a related cemetery. One, still within the city, was a Jewish cemetery near a synagogue. All the cemeteries, out of necessity, featured above ground family crypts that reminded me of New Orleans' macabre tourist's attractions.

The interior is characterized with scrublands, more closely resembling the Arizona high desert plains than a tropical island forest. The island is favored with cooling trade winds that keep the daytime temperatures in the low to mid-80s, and then in the evening bring warmer winds that keep the temperatures in the 70s. Along with the scruffy looking shrubs we saw several dominant forms of cacti, and witnessed multiple examples of how the cacti were cultivated into effective barrier fences around homes and small ranches and farms; primarily to keep goats and small donkeys inside but also as a deterrent to uninvited intruders. The tour guide was, however, quick to point out that the crime rate on Curacao was almost non-existent; and then segued to note reassuringly that because the island lies outside of the Caribbean hurricane belt Curacao is seldom affected directly by a significant storm. After three hours touring Curacao we returned to the ship.

That evening after we undocked at Curacao and slowly started on our way to Aruba, we had our customary drinks at the Diamond Lounge (lemon drops for Donna, and mostly wine for me), and later ate dinner. Then Donna went with our traveling couple's wife to a song and dance performance by the ships cast. I sat out on our balcony and wrote the first draft of the *Time Keeper*. I reworked and edited the *Time Keeper* several additional times while cruising on the *Navigator*, I had lines with arrows rearranging lines and referring to stanzas in later pages of my journal, a virtual labyrinth that no one other than I would ever be able to decode. Once home, I typed the latest draft on to our laptop and saved it to a removable disc. The *Time Keeper* poem, perhaps as much as anything I have written, reflects my soul's journey to my own, unique, middle path and provides an answer to the great conundrum—the question of God, and the purpose of life and humanity's place within the universe.

3/8/2017; Aruba

Another port of call in the Netherlands Dutch Antilles, another guided island tour; this time it is Aruba. Like Curacao, Aruba is an independent constituent country of the Kingdom of the Netherlands; a self-governing status also granted to St. Maarten by the Netherlands. The remaining Netherland Dutch Antilles islands, including Bonaire, remain possessions of the Kingdom; eschewing independence for their own reasons. Approximately twenty miles long and ten miles at its widest, Aruba is slightly larger in total square miles than is Curacao. The permanent population, around 100,000, is smaller than Curacao but significantly larger than Bonaire's population of 18,000. Aruba is situated less than twenty miles off the coast of Venezuela; all three of the series of Dutch islands that the *Navigator* had port calls at lie within a range of eleven to thirteen degrees north of the equator.

Of the ABC Islands, Donna and I agreed, Aruba most impressed us. The southern part of the island moving west to the capital city of Oranjestad is where you will find beautiful, white sandy beaches, and row upon row of luxury hotels catering to travelers vacationing for a week or two in Aruba. However, it was the intoxicatingly exotic northern and eastern coasts that excited our senses. These parts of the island are largely uninhabited. We saw rolling hills and sand dunes that looked like scenes from the Baja desert. Like Curacao, Aruba presented large areas of scrubland with thorny bushes, some evergreens, and cacti in abundance. Another plant, not native to Aruba, but that is cultivated on plantations and supports an entire industry is aloe (part of our tour stopped by an aloe plantation and processing facility). But it was the rugged northern and eastern coastline that most impressed. Here the island was buffeted by strong-armed ocean currents. Large waves twenty feet or higher crashed into the shore line, driven by an unrelenting prevailing trade wind, totally asserting natures absolute dominance. This contentious, relentless, wind was the driving force that coerced Aruba's watapana trees' trunks to bend nearly in half, away from its gale, and push all growth of the tree, also known as the divi-divi, in the direction of its path.

It was certain death to attempt to swim in this part of the islands' shoreline. At one stop, we visited the site of a large natural bridge that had collapsed in 2005. A smaller natural bridge survives nearby. Donna and I were drawn to the inlet that over eons had been carved out of volcanic rock and pumice. The thunderous sound of the pounding surf and the awesome power of the crashing waves sent mist upward and inland for a hundred or more yards and left us damp with a salty residue we could taste on our lips. I felt a spiritual connection with nature observing this wild, untamed part of the Caribbean.

Next up was Bonaire, but first I was on fire with inspiration from the primordial wildness that I experienced on Aruba. Tonight, I said to myself, I am compelled by some inner command to think again about the *God Particle* and to record those thoughts in my journal.

I had a burning desire to slay the dragon challenging my conviction that the Buddha's assertion that all is suffering and Kazantzakis' shout at the edge of the abyss were life affirming declarations. The Buddha's insight that all reality is constantly changing resonates with my own understanding of the natural world and our place within. To the Buddha, nothing stays the same, impermanence reigns supreme. Humans, as sensate beings, have a deep, primordial yearning for stability and permanence. Change (confronting suffering, sorrow, decay and death) is an anchor that weighs down the human spirit, and prevents it from climbing the steep, craggy ascent to a higher spiritual plane. Change, fear of change to be exact, is the final impediment to the transubstantiation of matter into spirit—to a higher state of awareness, to awakening and freedom. The Buddha's great awareness (I would say this applies with equal veracity to Kazantzakis) is to be awake to the realization that emptiness and its sibling, impermanence, does not diminish nor negate Joseph Campbell's notion of "bliss" and the enlightened insight of the Buddha that Nirvana is in this very moment, it is here, it is the Now.

I see, feel, hear and experience in the pilgrimages of the Buddha's life and Kazantzakis' *Spiritual Exercises*, a common thread of profound compassion and a sense of responsibility toward other humans—a social context and duty, secured in moral conduct (*sila*). This social context is Buddhism's Middle Path. Albert Schweitzer's writing about evil in the world evokes this same deep sense of compassion and sympathy: "Only at quite rare moments have I felt really glad to be alive. I could not but feel with a sympathy full of regret all the pain I saw around me, not only that of men, but of the whole creation." [7] It is the crux of Dante's dire condemnation for those who lack a moral compass and act outside of moral (right) conduct and stand by in silent acquiescence in the face of evil, such cowardly creatures are rejected by God and the Devil. Neither Kazantzakis or the Buddha would accept Dante's hell as real. But if reality only exists in the here and now, then truly each of them, I must conclude, would lament that neutrality in face of moral crisis (non-action) is paradise lost.

3/9/2017; Bonaire

The last port of call and last guided tour, before two sailing-days back to Miami, was Bonaire the smallest of the ABC islands, and to my mind the least memorable. Of the ABC islands, it is the furthest from the Venezuela coast. It occupies just over 100-square-miles of land and has a permanent population of about 18,000 people. The languages on Bonaire do not differ from Curacao and Aruba. Dutch is the official language, but other languages are common including a local hybrid dialect (Papiamentu), Spanish and English. All the ABC islands' public schools provide instruction in these languages and students are required to be proficient in all four. Permanent residents have access to government provided health care. Much of the southern part of Bonaire is flat and barely above sea level. This facilitates its use as a natural area that is employed in the commercial process of evaporating sea water and harvesting sea salt. The most interesting part of the tour was a stop in this region where small concrete slave huts were preserved. The huts had sloped roofs and small 24-inch square openings at the front and rear with concrete floors. When in use, before slavery was abolished in the 1860's, two to three slaves slept in the huts which were about four feet tall (excluding the roof) and had approximately 5 by 6 feet of floor space. The huts resembled small open-ended burial crypts. Donna and I looked at each other wondering what loss of humanity is involved with the enslavement of other humans. Slavery has been a scourge upon the collective soul of humanity. It has been a plague that has followed mankind since antiquity. Humans have been subjected to slavery and its insidious cruelty from conquests by invaders and conscriptions by royalty. The African slave trade that lasted for several centuries in the Americas was fueled by greed and lust for wealth and employed to sustain otherwise unprofitable commercial enterprises. The American experience wrought a civil war and nearly tore apart our country. It has been called "the peculiar institution" but that label does not suffice. Slavery is evil, and its existence is a blight upon our history. There may only be one abomination eviler than slavery—genocide. The systematic extermination of people based upon their culture, religion or race is humanity's darkest, most loathsome, depraved act. Here, too, our country cannot come to the table with clean hands. The genocide campaigns conducted against the native American Indian tribes was horrific, homicidal, and repulsive. Today, despite history's lessons, the world is not free of slavery; whether it is in the form of human trafficking or subtler economic exploitation. So, too, the lessons of our government's attempts to exterminate the American Indian tribes, and the Nazi Holocaust that systematically killed six million European Jews, have not brought an end to crimes against humanity in Europe, Africa, Asia, and South America. Sadly, hatred and bigotry still fuel the fires of genocide.

3/10/2017; sailing back to Miami

I spent several hours, once the sun had set, on our balcony gazing at the ocean. I was not in a trance, but you could say I was mesmerized by the sea. Later that evening I wrote some observations in my journal. As I stare upon the ocean, I see the rolling waves and the white caps giving subtle hints of surface changes. Yet beneath, in the ocean's great depths, nothing that I could discern, stirred. There in the impenetrable darkness, the ocean's nature remained essentially undiscoverable and unknown. So, too, I thought, is the *God Particle*. On the surface, we glimpse its subtle manifestations. We look introspectively inside ourselves, and outwardly to others; our loved ones, neighbors, and other humans continents away. We examine religious thought, and the writings of seers, philosophers, poets, playwrights and novelists. We peer into the messages and meanings provided by wise, great souls who offer insights—glimpses into the unknown. We search in vain for any clue within these surface changes. We search for answers for ourselves, for all humanity, for all the creatures of the earth; and for forces of life that cannot think for themselves or others—the planets, the stars and the galaxies that populate the universe. But the ocean depth defies our inquiry and does not reveal itself. In the end, it is unfathomable, impenetrable, and inscrutable; lying beyond the limits of human comprehension. The conundrum still exists, I said to myself. Perhaps, as has been suggested, the Buddha addressed this dilemma best by seeking the solution to life's puzzle within the self and leaving the cosmos to resolve its mystery on its own. The mystery persists and although our languages cannot articulate the unknowable, our intuition can enlighten and illuminate a path. The following morning, I drew upon those thoughts to write the poem *A Depth Too Deep to See*.

3/11/2017

This was our last full day a sea. We were cruising back to Miami. I wrote *A Depth Too Deep to See,* finished entries in my journal for the *Navigator* cruise with the following observation:

It is a pathway of endless struggle and ascent to transform matter into spirit. This, not the mystery surrounding the catholic doctrine of the Eucharist, where bread and wine are transformed, by priestly intervention, into the body and blood of Christ, is the true miracle of transubstantiation. This is the awakening that the Buddha and Nikos Kazantzakis shared with me on our cruise. I opened my mind. I allowed them to intrude and disrupt what little comfort remained in my psyche, and I awoke and was free.

Anticipation

4/2/2017

Donna and I will soon begin packing for our next cruise, a twelve-day sail out of Bayonne, New Jersey, bound for the Caribbean on Royal Caribbean's

An Essay on the Question of God

Anthem of the Seas, embarking on April 17. I will turn 70 on that cruise; we will celebrate that day at one of the giant ship's specialty restaurants of my choice.

As I completed the editing and transcription of the writing I accomplished on the *Navigator* cruise, I have turned my attention to reworking a 35-year-old unpublished literary analysis of Nikos Kazantzakis' The Saviors of God. Unless I decide later to attempt to refashion an unfinished lengthy poem on John the Baptist into a short story and include it in my yet completed book Oh God, Where Art Thou? The Great Conundrum, the literary analysis will complete the book.

Port Liberty New Jersey; April 17, 2017

Donna and I board Royal Caribbean Cruise Line's (RCCL) *Anthem of the Seas* for a twelve-day cruise to eastern Caribbean islands that include St. Kitts, St. Maarten, Martinique, Barbados, Antigua and Puerto Rico. We are traveling with neighbors and great friends, seasoned sea travelers, who also come to help celebrate my 70th birthday occurring while we cruise. We have two full sea days sailing to San Juan, then five straight days after docking daily at an island before a journey of three days at sea back to Port Liberty, in Bayonne. This will differ somewhat from our *Navigator* cruise in March because Donna and I have been to all these islands before and we will likely do beaches rather than tours, shopping or just walking near the pier and sampling the local culinary fair. Neither of us are great swimmers but we love wading in the clear Caribbean waters with its soft white sand and lounging on chairs underneath a beach umbrella sipping bottled water and some island specialty beverage or a Caribbean beer.

The *Anthem* was launched in 2015. It is one RCCL's newer, large Quantum-class ships in its fleet. It is over 167,800 gross tons, 1,141 feet long and 136 feet wide, has 18 decks, has a top speed of 22 knots (25 miles per hour), and has a passenger capacity of 4,180 (double occupancy) and 4,900 total guests, and carries an international crew of nearly 1,500. It has all the amenities that newer, large cruise ships offer including RCCL's unique North Star, a glass observational pod that takes guests 300 feet in the air and rotates over the sides of the ship to provide an amazing 360-degree venue with views of the ship's top decks and ocean.

Sailing; April 18, 2017

I sat out on our balcony for a while to think about what I yet needed to accomplish to finalize my manuscript Oh God, Where Art Thou? The Great Conundrum. It is 68 degrees and a bit cool on our stateroom balcony as we are about as far south as northern North Carolina, approximately 850 miles from first docking in San Juan. I intend to finish, for a third read, but first in five years, Kazantzakis' autobiography A Report to Greco. I have determined that there are primary sources from the author himself that I should weave into my literary analysis of Kazantzakis' The Saviors of God. I also plan to add some to the travel accounts and, if inspiration comes, perhaps I'll find the creative urge to write another poem to build into the manuscript's portfolio of poetry.

Sailing; April 19, 2017

I continued reading the final chapters of Report to Greco. I concluded that it is important for anyone who eventually might read my book that they have the author's personal perspective on why I chose to write Oh God, Where Art Thou? The Great Conundrum; this essay woven into a travel journal, its poetry meant to be dramatically heard more so than merely read, its short stories revived from early immature efforts, and the literary analysis [later to be abandoned] of the book that to me forms a sacred text of a set of "spiritual exercises" and the process-oriented ethics that I believe is lost in these times of great strife, political distress, environmental threats, and the erosion of social and economic justice in the face of unbridled greed and avarice.

My career, I would humbly offer, has been as a skilled practitioner of higher education administration. I have spent a working lifetime communicating with and among administrators, boards, commissions, lawyers, the media, politicians, legislators, and scholarly faculty. However, I am not a learned scholar of the Buddha, or Kazantzakis and the powerful influences (Bergson, Nietzsche, Christ and the Buddha) who affected Kazantzakis' evolving philosophy of life, and his "Cretan Glance" at life's inscrutable creator and life's inherent sacred purpose. But the Buddha and Nikos Kazantzakis have been my constant intellectual companions and protagonists; prodding my skeptical, cynical mind and my slowly maturing psyche to search endlessly across the span of my life for a solution to the Great Conundrum—the question of God. I know them. I have internalized them. I have ingested them; not as an academic, but as my soul's captain. They have driven me to search through observation, experience, rationality, logic, and finally intuition—in an endless pursuit for a satisfying answer, for a resting perch, for some place or thought anchored in certainty. As soon as I seemed to find an answer that might be sufficient, the sand beneath my feet would shift, and the comforting salve of hope would be washed away. Until now, at long last, as I write and let go of the fool's gold of treasured hope. Now awake, I see and feel with all my senses life's affirming truth. Life, so simple and sublime, is its own intrinsic worth. It needs no hope for a reward or fear of some punishment; no need to eternally recur; no necessity for an enduring self. Its heroic, defiant, journey has always been and is its validating joy and purpose, substantial enough for the brave and to those who obtain the blissful awareness of the awakened.

This, and the awareness of my age never as before, is the root cause, the driving force and obsessive compulsion to put on paper thoughts long trapped within my insatiably, unaccepting, ruminating mind. These are no longer my thoughts only, prisoners within my mind. They are there for anyone to inspect. One or a thousand, it does not matter. I give them freely to others, to anyone; to ponder, to consider, to embrace, to criticize, or to reject.

Art Auction; April 19, 2017

Later in the afternoon Donna and I attended a Park West Gallery art auction (they are a feature on all Royal Caribbean Cruise Line sailings). We bid and purchased an Anatoly Metlan painting of a playful, dancing woman in a red dress, entitled *To Her Own Beat II*. This is an early 70th birthday gift for Donna who does not turn seventy until March of 2018. The painting reminds me of my beloved wife. Beautiful, alive with joy and happiness, full of compassion and charity, in frenzied, jubilant dance—that is Donna in her essence. She is the lighter spirit. I am the brooding, obsessed thinker. Every day for the rest of my life when I pass by that colorful painting, I will smile, my soul will sigh, and I will feel a sense of peace and comfort that will fill that moment with pure, blissful happiness.

April 20, 2017

As we neared the island of Puerto Rico, the water took on a green luster; not deep like spring grass, but lighter, typical of grass in late fall along the Atlantic coast from Virginia north to New York and inland to the Midwest through Ohio all the way to Illinois. Puerto Rico, a self-governing

Commonwealth of the United States, is 110 miles long and 40 miles wide, with a total population of about 3.4 million permanent residents. Although larger than many Caribbean islands, it is the smallest of the Greater Antilles; smaller by some than Jamaica, and less than 10 percent the size of Cuba.

San Juan, its capital, with a population of 400,000 residents, was established in 1508; the second oldest established city in the New World and home to the tomb of Ponce de Leon, the explorer and searcher for the mythic Fountain of Youth. It is noted for two formidable military forts that are now dominate tourist sites, San Cristobal and El Morro which cruise ships pass on their way to dock and allow passengers to debark. The city contrasts modern five-story hotels and ten-story office buildings, with the old forts and churches, cobblestone streets, and mountains and tropical rain forests that loom outside the city in the island's interior. [Note this obviously predates hurricane Maria.]

I sat that night on the balcony reflecting on how best to explain why I reject some of poetry's conventional constraints. I struggled for a proper explanation, then the quiet ocean once again provided that semi-conscious state of reflection when inspiration and intellect couple, followed by creation. Finally, the seed I planted germinated. I had my explanation. Imagine for a moment, a small, sparrow-like bird caught in a hunter's snare. Trembling, the tiny creature is removed gently into two large waiting hands. Its heart is beating furiously, to the point of bursting. Captive, constrained within the hunter's hands, it is a prisoner of uncertainty, fearful of what might happen next. Is it injury, death, or escape and flight to freedom? A kaleidoscope of possibilities occupies its small struggling mind, all tied to the tiny creature's trepidation and the specter of unfolding pain and suffering, and the spirit crushing threat of imminent death. And here, at this point, as its creator I chose release, flight and freedom for the captive bird.

I grant myself, with no permission from those who believe in rules of rhyme, meter, stanza, numbered lines, and syntax, the freedom of flight from all such constraint. If these rules suppress my own creative urge and leave thoughts unexpressed, trapped within my mind, then I am the poorer soul for acquiescing to convention's limitations. Like the little bird that I created; I, too, chose freedom, not caring what critics and any reader might later have to say.

April 21, 2017; a milestone birthday

An amazing moment just unfolded. I woke up in the morning and I was 70 years into my life's journey. Our precious time races by inexorably; look back and the voyage from childhood, through adolescence, adulthood, and then to aging maturity passes nearly imperceptibly.

We arrive in St. Maarten at 10:30 in the morning. St. Maarten is the Dutch part of the Island of Saint Martin. It enjoys autonomy within the Kingdom of the Netherlands. It is located on the southern half of the island. Our ship docks at its capital, Philipsburg. To the north is the French part of the island. Together the two separately governed sections of the island total 37 square miles.

I started off with daily exercise in the ship's fitness center. At 5:30 a.m. when I opened our stateroom door, I was greeted with balloons and a poster that had three photos; a collaboration between Donna and the wife of our traveling companions and great friends. One photo was of me at age three, another was me at age 19 taken in Tripoli with Ajax, my military sentry dog. The third photo was me at age 68, taken at Millersville University's Biemesderfer Executive Center during my university retirement reception. Later, when we are docked, the four of us will take a taxi to a beach to wade, sun and relax. Then in the evening Donna and I will have drinks, hors d'oeuvres, and conversation with our dear traveling friends and new shipmate acquaintances, before going to a specialty restaurant for a birthday dinner celebration.

In the morning, after exercise, Donna and I enjoyed breakfast on our balcony. In the distance, we saw a small sail boat as our ship, traveling at 18 knots, cruised on toward St. Maarten. Had we disturbed a sailor's solitude? Had our large ship intruded on a seafarer's ride across the ocean's waves? What was it doing, where was it headed we asked each other. It appeared to be so far out to sea, and so small; white sails and mast barely visible above its companion white-capped, three-foot waves, that moved with the rocking boat like a vast school of very large fish.

Later, around 8 a.m., we had our first sight of birds in several days. A small flock of ten to twelve white bodied, gray wing tipped sea gulls glided alongside the *Anthem*—our feathered, in flight, escorts to St. Maarten's port. Their shrill, caw-caw sounds communicating some instinctive, imprinted genetic code, a communal alert that the large sea disrupting vessel would soon stir schools of bite-sized, lazy fish from their relative peace and present life's sustaining opportunity for the birds to feed their hungry appetites.

Philosophy

Then the gulls would have the fuel they would need for their recurring labor of flight, glide and dive.

April 22, 2017; St. John's Antigua

Antigua is one of the Caribbean Leeward Islands. Its largest city is St. John with a population of approximately 32,000 people; the total island population is about 88,000. Antigua disassociated itself from Great Britain in 1981 and became an independent state within the Commonwealth of Nations. It was originally settled by indigenous people from South America, including the Arawak people from present day Venezuela. Conquered and exploited by European colonists the island was home to sugar plantations and slavery until abolished by Great Britain in the early 1800's. Today, tourism is the main economy buttressed with 365 beaches, all open to the public. We spent the early afternoon in the water and sun at Dickenson Bay Beach.

April 23, 2017; Martinique and more writing

We docked at Fort de France. A French island, Martinique is a larger island than I initially recalled as I heard the captain say during his daily morning update that the island was about 50 miles long and 10 miles wide (more like 43 miles long and 19 miles wide). It was a beautiful day, but I needed some rest and we stayed on the ship; five daily port calls in a row are a bit much, especially if you are a member of the baby-boomer generation and tend to be beach goers. [Later, in 2018 I learned that I had severe aortic stenosis. Subsequently, I had aortic valve replacement surgery and my energy levels are on the upswing.]

That evening, while working from our balcony, I added more material to this journal. I can't say what triggered my mind to think about a human peculiarity, but I admit I have thought about this human trait from time to time. Perhaps it was the moon's reflection on the ocean. I am intrigued that man is the only creature on earth, that I am aware of, endowed with a brain that enables us to see ourselves functioning in our environment. With our eyes we can see, and with our minds watch, observe and reflect upon our bodies movements within the space we inhabit. The mind's visual recognition of its body in its environment is fascinating. This sighting and recognition of our selves within our environment is a true out of body experience. Amazing.

An Essay on the Question of God

A passage from a later chapter in Nikos Kazantzakis' Report to Greco piqued my interest and caused me to reflect on my own ancestors and their ancestral burial site. Kazantzakis wrote: "Men can find no religious awe more genuine and profound, I believe, than the awe he feels when treading upon ground where his ancestors—his roots—repose. Your own feet sprout roots which descend into the earth and search, seeking to mingle with the great, immortal roots of the dead."[8]

The Home Cemetery, nestled in a small obscure corner in Youngstown, Ohio's 2,500-acre Mill Creek Park, has always affected my own soul in this same acutely aware way. I have often said that I feel a deep sense of connection, a renewal of spirit when I tread upon the soil that cradles the remains of generations of my ancestors. There, buried beneath my feet, I can walk across the resting places of family that stretches for generations, more than two centuries of ancestral lifetimes.

I had the same experience and sensations when I returned to my parent's home, after both had passed away. They died within six months of each other. Married over 50 years, they each died at the age of eighty. Their home, our home, my brother's and sister's home, my home was never merely a house. It was always home, a haven, a place where my perpetually restless soul could find a landing perch and have time to pause and rest.

It seemed so empty when I would stay during a visit before it was sold, and our parent's small humble estate was divided equally among their five children; three boys and two girls spanning 20 years between the oldest and the youngest sibling. My mother was the last to pass away. My father died six months before, and he died about a year after our niece, Erin, succumbed to a rare incurable brain tumor. That was a trying 18-month period of death and loss for our family. But the few times I stayed after they were gone, I still felt the warmth of a homecoming. I could feel the heat and smell the aromas of food cooking in the tiny kitchen. My mother could do wonders with a simple pot roast and mashed potatoes. We still talk about her made from scratch sweet and sour salad dressing and summertime potato and macaroni salads; no one made them better. I recalled the frequent, large, extended family gatherings filled wonderful, substantial meals, interesting conversations, and children playing games. During those lonely visits, just a few in number, I experienced the sensation of belonging to something larger than myself, to something spanning generations—present, gone, and yet to come.

Philosophy

At those times, and still today, my ancestors live while I live, and I can resurrect them in my mind. This process was real for the brooding, obsessed thinker who, from early adolescence, had abandoned all hope of an enduring self. Their rebirth, their moments in eternity were resurrected from death's dread grasp; just for that interluding moment when my ruminating mind recalled and brought them back to life. The mind's eyes keep them alive, for a single generation they remain with me, part of our collective soul. Death's fear of nothingness postponed, but only for a moment, only until I too pass and my journey with mother earth comes to its own end.

April 24, 2017; Barbados

Barbados, an independent British Commonwealth nation since 1966, has a population of about 275,000 people. The island is 21 miles long and 14 miles wide. Like many Caribbean islands, it was first populated as early as the 4th century by indigenous peoples from the Americas. The Spanish conquered the island in the early 1500's. The British took possession of the island in 1625 and later it became a British colony. In twisted irony, the sugar cane industry that started in the mid-1600 hundreds relied on imported slaves from Africa while inquisition persecuted Jews fled Europe to Barbados. Today, tourism is the main economic sector with visitors coming in highest numbers from the United Kingdom, the United States, and Canada. We spent the day at the Dockyard Beach where the water was as beautiful, clear, with gentle waves, and the sand was white and soft—this made for a refreshing, relaxing day at the beach.

April 25, 2017; St. Kitts

I have written about St. Kitts before. It is among our most favored Caribbean islands to visit. Donna and I love the Mountains, the always cloud shrouded dormant volcano (at least every time we have been in port). But with an unfavorable weather forecast, and heavy clouds and early morning rain, we canceled our beach plans and stayed on board the *Anthem*. To non-cruisers this might seem like a wasted day, but to people like Donna and I, there is always much to do on board. We enjoy sea days on the floating five-star resorts nearly as much as our island excursions. This fall we are flying to Barcelona, Spain; touring for four days and then boarding RCCL's

An Essay on the Question of God

Freedom of the Seas for a fourteen-day transatlantic cruise that includes stops at three Canary Islands before its seven-day Atlantic crossing.

Cruising home; April 26–29

The sight of that lone skiff became the inspiration for the poem that occupied my creative energy for much of the remaining cruise. When we were back, docked in Port Liberty, I had written draft three of *The Watchman's Gaze*, and would add it into my manuscript. I would type and finalize the poem once I was home. Then, I resolved, to focus attention on my literary analysis and weave in some primary source material direct from Kazantzakis' Report to Greco, complete the necessary work on the footnote section, and then begin to explore the world of publication.

August 28, 2017; Update

I have since finished the literary analysis and am seeking permission to quote extensively, a prerequisite for a thoughtful literary analysis, from the apparent copyright holder of Kazantzakis' The Saviors of God manuscript. In addition, I now have eight poems and three short stories rounding out my manuscript, and work toward publication.

November 29, 2017; Mount Joy, Pennsylvania

Plans change with time and circumstances. I have waited several months but have not secured, in fact not heard back at all, permission from the copyright holder of The Saviors of God. Silence can never be inferred as acceptance, in seeking permission to advance with fair copyright use; and how much more for matters sexual as daily news accounts unfold acts that run a gamut from poor taste, to power's gross abuse, and on to vile pedophiles depraved pursuit preying on children like craven beasts. Consequently, I have to move on and simply remove the literary analysis of Kazantzakis' ethical based philosophical treatise from my manuscript. The effort is not a total loss as his work has served as an inspirational anchor for the development of my own philosophical perspective on the nature of the cosmos and our place within. Meanwhile, I have had to find a suitable replacement for the literary analysis and have turned to poetry to fill that void. I am at work on a long narrative tale entitled *No Time for Remorse: Another Tale of Voices in Verse*. The title is a tribute to Robert Penn Warren's tale in verse and voices

Brothers to Dragons. My work is a panoramic American political perspective and commentary on our country's bumpy but progressive evolutionary path toward a more pluralistic, egalitarian society, and the challenges that have unfolded, especially in the current political landscape. I am more than half way through the outline I developed for writing this narrative tale in blank verse. I hope to finish the work by the spring of 2018.

In the interim since our Anthem of the Seas cruise Donna and I traveled to Barcelona, Spain, and after five days of visiting Barcelona highlights boarded Freedom of the Seas for a 14-day transatlantic cruise with port calls in Cadiz, and three of the Canary Islands prior to a seven-day journey across the Atlantic to Fort Lauderdale. While on board Freedom I wrote another poem that has been added to my manuscript entitled *The Last Judgment*. The poem is a plea to reconsider for those who think of suicide and is a counter point to Dante's dark view of the hellish fate that awaits the suicidal from an avenging God whose vengeful divine punishment is reserved for those poor souls who deprive Dante's all-just God of his grand design. For Dante, and the Catholic Church of his time (and even so today), it was the ego of their God that he and only he could decide how each and every living soul must die. No one, they asserted had a moral right to stop the life that this great creator had given them, not before their god sent his ferryman to gather up their soul.

We enjoyed trips to wineries in Barcelona, Cadiz, and the Gran Canaries where we visited the active volcano of Mt. Teide on the island of Tenerife with its sulfur fumes and bubbling hot liquid pools, and the Gran Canarias where we traveled to the interior up approximately 4,000 feet to a coffee and orange plantation and winery for the most remarkable tapas and wine tasting experience of our life at Bodega Los Berrazales. But Barcelona stole our hearts. We loved strolling Los Ramblas where the Catalonians were gracious and friendly despite the ongoing peaceful protests for independence from Spain. However, we discovered it was the French and the destruction the invading army of Napoleon who the Catalonians most resented. The passion of Catalonian dislike for the French invaders is intensely experienced when visiting Montserrat.

Approximately 4,000 feet high at St. Jerome, its highest peak, Montserrat is the craggy, saw toothed mountain 10 kilometers long. To me it resembled a giant dragon as our bus twisted and turned up the ascending mountain road to the Benedictine monastery, with origins to the 12th century, which later in the 16th century was home to the religious icon of the Black Madonna within the beautiful basilica near the monk's cloister which dates back to the 15th century. The complex nearly destroyed by the Napoleonic invaders was restored beginning in the 19th century. We stayed for the beginning of a Catholic Mass that featured Gregorian chants from the thirty or so Benedictine monks that still lived in the restored cloister. Before leaving Donna lit two candles for the sick daughter of friends, and for loved ones passed. I respect her beliefs although we do not share them in common, but I will confess that the entire experience at Montserrat was humbling and inspiring, a tribute to human ingenuity, passion and creativity.

Nothing, however, surpassed the moveable spiritual feast we experienced on our leisurely, awe-struck tour of the incredible Sagrada Familia; the architectural wonder envisioned by the genius of Antonia Gaudi and his use of nature motifs in the design and structural engineering of his tribute to the Holy Family. Gaudi envisioned, designed, and oversaw the early construction, until his death in 1926, of what is one of the most remarkable cathedrals human minds have conceived and worked to create. The central temple complex of Sagrada Familia is supported by enormous tree like columns that support the center cathedral dome that rests nearly 600 feet from the main floor. Stain glass windows are portals for the natural light of the day to dazzle the eyes with the sun's changing path and its varying effects on the palette of colors that penetrate and paint the interior of the cathedral. The sculptures are bold, modernistic portrayals of three themes attached to the holy family; each featured in one of the three facades for entry into the architectural and artistic wonder that is Sagrada Familia. The sunrise positioned Nativity Façade with its trumpeting angels signals the birth of Christ and in larger context the birth of life itself. The Passion Façade which faces west, and the setting sun is topped with a naked, crucified Christ hanging from the cross with Adam's skull at the base of the cross, for whose original sin God has sacrifice his only son in atonement. The Glory Façade, a tribute to Christ's resurrection and conquest over death, is still a work in progress. The hope is that it will be finished sometime between 2026–2028, nearly 150 years after its initial ground breaking. The giant bronze doors to the Glory Façade feature the Lord's Prayer carved in 50 languages. You cannot visit, walk about, and observe this wonder of the modern world without feeling humble, spiritually uplifted, and enthralled with man's ingenuity and creativity.

Philosophy

Final Summary; May 14, 2018

Three more cruises, three more times to meditate and contemplate, three more times to find inspiration to write. In that time, I wrote *The Old Home Cemetery, The Wolf's Lament, Who Hears the Silence of My Sounds* (a tribute to our granddaughter Claire, for her courage and bravery, as every day this strong 12-year-old wages her own personal war with Tourette's Syndrome and Obsessive-Compulsive Disorder), and ultimately completed the other anchor to Oh God, Where Art thou? The Great Conundrum, the afore mentioned epic tale in voices and verse *No Time for Remorse*.

In that interim, I also read a news report about the fascinating concept of biocentrism. Now, I don't pretend to have this theory exactly figured out. But I believe some of my thoughts and writing have been coincidental efforts that has drawn out the contours of hybrid concepts of my limited understanding of this intriguing theory of the universe, our perceptual experience of time and space, and the implications this might have on the prevailing construct of our conception of the phenomenon of life and death. In shorthand, the theory plays out like this: the consciousness of sensate beings paints the canvas of reality through which life itself unfolds in a series of distinct, irreducible, indestructible, infinite moments. Everything exists only in the moment, the 'now' that our consciousness enables us to perceive. This new focus on biocentrism, and how this concept opens up new insights into our outmoded perspective of the time-space continuum, and the very notion of death, has helped my physics challenged brain gain a better instinctive grasp into the continuing mystery of time and space, which at some subconscious level must have resonated with my own evolving notion of a series of individually constructed universes that are the work product of sensate minds. The question begged is, is there actually a quintillion time a quintillion time (an infinity, if you will) of universes that are made possible in the consciousness of an infinite number of sensate beings' minds?

I captured some of this in my writing, even if I did not know or recognize it at its moment of creation. I reflect back and recall that in writing about the *God Particle*, I speculated that even if my own perceptual experiences did not exist, then they had to exist within the framework of some cognitive, sensate stream of consciousness belonging to someone else's awareness, dreams or illusions. Now, I question that construct as imperfectly expressed. I think the dialogue I created between the Buddha and the mystery man in *No Time for Remorse* illuminate a parallel framework that demonstrates an intuitive grasp of the broader contours of this fresh look at time, space, and the place of life and death therein. Here is that dialogue:

> *You must find your bliss in the keen awareness*
>
> *That man, the thinker who created God; the we*
>
> *With all our senses of sight, and sound and touch,*
>
> *Will never fathom the how or why of creation's*
>
> *Confounding mystery. This enigma is unsettling,*
>
> *It is the great conundrum that even the God*
>
> *Of human ingenuity may never understand or know.*
>
> *Perhaps the teacher you adore, best says it right,*
>
> *Captured in the wisdom of his tome that spoke*
>
> *Heroically of the fearless Cretan saviors of the gods,*
>
> *Who bore the heavy burden bravely, and did not acquiesce*
>
> *To hope, or seek in terror to refute the sublime*
>
> *Closing line that questions existence as a reality . . . .*
>
> *Then as ready as I could be, I said to the Buddha:*
>
> *"some say that hell is the eternal separation*
>
> *Of an undeserving man from his just god,*
>
> *But, to me, the bitter often unobserved irony,*
>
> *Is that man and his many fickle gods,*
>
> *And the grandeur of the universe, exist together,*
>
> *Only in the consciousness of a single human mind.*

I leave you with these thoughts and questions. The Buddha had his profound moment of "awareness" in contemplation beneath the Bodhi Tree. I had my own moment of insight and awareness, perhaps of less profundity, in cumulative sessions of contemplation on the balconies of ships cruising the Atlantic and Pacific Oceans and the Caribbean and Mediterranean Seas. Thought different in environment, their essential essence was the same: natural, quiet, peaceful and generally removed from the clatter and noise of ordinary circumstances, as well as news of calamities. My mind continues to churn on the awareness that the universe may exist only through the lenses of a single sensate being, each of us a god of creation in our own right. Our senses of observation, intuition, intellect, art and instinct are the tools we have to craft the universe as it exists only through our individual cognitive perceptions. This does not render existence an empty exercise of survival in the void of nothingness. A moral compass, right conduct, human empathy and compassion for all life place a defiant stamp of nobility on the universe as we perceive it. But without the observation of a sensate being, the universe is silent, static, unperceived, nonexistent. If there is no one able to witness the transpiring of a moment, to act consciously within that moment, then there is no moment that has transpired. This is my "awareness." Look for yours within yourself, within the brace of the kinsmen of humanity, and the animals and plants that nurture and sustain life on this tiny planet earth. Look for yours in the face of our sun, the living, burning orb which warms the earth like a child held within a blanket in its mother's arms safe from winter's chill. Look for yours wherever the great arc of creation and moral conduct intersect, and act within that cauldron of uncertainty. I have my answer. Do you? Does a tree make noise as it falls if there is no one there to hear? Does a giant, dying, exploding star matter on some galactic scale if there is no sensate being in search of its mystery?

References for the Essay

1. Jorge Mario Bergoglio, Pope Francis, *"Evangelii Gaudium," No to the new idolatry of money*, (Vatican 2013) p. 174.
2. Dante Alighieri, *The Inferno*, canto iii, lines 35–41, *The Divine Comedy* translated by Henry Wadsworth Longfellow, (Leipzig, 1867), p.178
3. F. Max Muller, *The Way of the Buddha*, translated from Pali, (New York, 2008), p.186.
4. Robert Penn Warren, *Brothers to Dragons, A Tale in Verse and Voices, A New Version*, (LSU Press Edition, 1966), p. 186.
5. Huston Smith, *The World's Religions*, Harper Collins Publisher, (New York, 1991), p.187.
6. Nikos Kazantzakis, *The Saviors of God: Spiritual Exercises*, Translated, with an Introduction by Kimon Friar, Simon & Schuster, (New York,1960), p.187.
7. Albert Schweitzer, *An Anthology*, edited by Charles Rhiad Joy, Enlarged Edition, Beacon Press, (Boston, 1956), p.192.
8. Nikos Kazantzakis, *Report to Greco*, Translated by P.A. Bein with Introduction by Helen Kazantzakis, (New York, 1965), p.201.

Resources for the Manuscript

1. *Abraham Lincoln, the Prairie Years and War Years*, Carl Sandburg, Harcourt & Brace, (New York, 1954).
2. *The Complete Works of William Shakespeare, with the Temple Notes*, World, (Cleveland, 1900).
3. *Good News for Modern Man*, The New Testament in Today's English Version, American Bible Association, 3rd Edition, (New York, 1971).
4. *Holy Bible*, New Revised Standard Version, Augsburg Fortress, (Minneapolis, 1990).
5. *Jefferson*, Saul K. Padover, Harcourt & Brace, (New York, 1980).
6. *The Prophet*, Kahlil Gibran, Jaico Publishing House, (Mumbai, 2011).
7. *Team of Rivals*, Doris Kearns Goodwin, Simon & Schuster, (New York, 2005).
8. *Theodore Rex*, Edmund Morris, Random House, (New York, 2001).
9. "William Faulkner's 1949 Nobel Prize in Literature Acceptance Speech," *Literature: 1901–1967 (Nobel Lectures in Literature)*, (v. 1), Horst Frenz, Elsevier.

www.ingramcontent.com/pod-product-compliance
Lightning Source LLC
Chambersburg PA
CBHW060605230426
43670CB00011B/1978